I MADE A
SHORT FILM
NOW WTF DO
I DO WITH IT

A GUIDE TO FILM FESTIVALS, PROMOTION, AND SURVIVING THE RIDE

CLARISSA JACOBSON

SUNBURY PRESS

Mechanicsburg, PA USA

Published by Sunbury Press, Inc.
Mechanicsburg, Pennsylvania

www.sunburypress.com

ISBN: 978-1-62006-338-5 (Trade paperback)

Library of Congress Control Number: 2019951441

FIRST SUNBURY PRESS EDITION: October 2019

Product of the United States of America
0 1 1 2 3 5 8 13 21 34 55

Set in Bookman Old Style
Designed by Rebecca Kelleher Design
(rkelleherdesign.com)
Cover by Hallie Brown
Edited by Lawrence Knorr

Continue the Enlightenment!

ACKNOWLEDGMENTS

This book is dedicated to:

My father, author *Cliff Jacobson*, who always tells me *"you can do it!"*; my mom, Sharon, who isn't here anymore but was my biggest cheerleader; and my mentor *Joe Bratcher* who taught me to write and guides me on my artistic journey.

I would also like to thank:
Jeffrey Fiterman, who is always there for me; *Beve Roman*, who helps me be brave even when I'm afraid; *Peggy Farrell* with her big heart, who always believes in me; *Shayna Weber*, who makes me laugh and has great ideas; *Bev Nero*, for her wonderful, infectious optimism; *Judy Farrell*, who supports artists' dreams; *Chuti Tiu*, for being awesomely relentless and fixing my commas; *Twin Bridges Writing Salon*, who gives me the best writing notes and is my favorite place to visit every week; *Mike & Rebecca Kelleher*, who are generous beyond belief; and the whole team on my short film *Lunch Ladies*—especially set designers *Alicia* and *Ray Ho*, SFX guru *Matt Falletta* and director, *J.M. Logan*, who said—*"hey you learned so much about festivals and promotion from* Lunch Ladies—*you should write a book!"*

Cover Design by *Hallie Brown*, whom I met on
Instagram and who drew the first fan art ever for
Lunch Ladies.

TABLE OF CONTENTS

PROLOGUE

Congratulations! You are amazing!

You dared to dream, dared to make a film, raised that money, saved that money, pinched, squeezed and bled that money, slaved over scripts, locations, long nights, early mornings, fears, hopes, worries, argued with the negative voice inside your head and came out alive. Not only alive, but you finished your masterpiece and it's awesome.

Now, WTF do you do with it?

Well, amazing person, I was you once. I, too, didn't know the first thing about promoting a film or getting it on the circuit. I'd heard the tales—that politics matter, how the odds are stacked against you, what types of films are successful, what types aren't . . .

In short, I knew the word on the street—why you couldn't succeed vs. why you could.

However, I don't listen to that stuff, and neither should you—it does not serve you. First lesson, whenever anything negative comes your way (and there will be a lot), ask if it serves your film; if it doesn't, ignore. That will serve you. But I digress.

Anyhow, I knew the word on the street—why you couldn't succeed vs. why you could.

But I also knew my film was terrific (and you must know this too about your film or you've lost already) and I had a goal (get ready for *Chapter 1*).

I therefore learned everything I could, battled the haters, battled my insecurities, didn't give up on my short, believed in it, kept my eyes on the prize, worked like crazy and had an amazing run: over one hundred film festivals all over the world, more than thirty awards, gold standard distribution, over eighty reviews/interviews and a wide fan base.

To be clear, for all you folks who think I had a leg up in ANY way—I didn't. This was my first film. I had very few connections; no one on the circuit knew my work or me (Clarissa who?) and I had a film that didn't fit the mold (a comedy/horror genre piece coming in at the appalling length of 19 minutes).

Still. It. Succeeded.

I want you to succeed too and I'm going to pass on all the things that I learned: how to promote, how to submit to festivals, how to maximize your fest budget, how to think big, how to overcome negativity, how to laugh at rejections, how to love social media, how to get filmmaker discounts and more. Let's get started!

CHAPTER 1

GET A GOAL OR BE A GONER

(preliminary first step to keep you focused)

I know this probably makes you feel like you're back in junior high, and I'm that really annoying teacher who's on your case, but seriously:

> **"What is your goal, what are you gonna do with your film? Focus ya delinquent!"**

Trust me, kids, having a goal is gonna make everything so much easier. You put so much time into making your short, but the true marathon is the next eighteen months after you've finished it. There will be a massive amount of work to do to give it a life.

If you look around at the films that succeed it's not just about quality (there are thousands of good flicks that never see the light of day and plenty of bad ones that do), it is also about the filmmaker's goal—knowing what they want to achieve.

- *Some people make short films just to create. Is that you?*
- *Some people make short films to practice their craft. Is that you?*
- *Some people make short films to get interest in their career. Is that you?*

- *Some people make short films as a proof-of-concept for their feature. Is that you?*
- *Some people make short films because they can't afford to make long ones. Is that you?*
- *Some people make short films because . . .*

You get my drift.

Figure out why you made your film. When you figure out why you made it, you can figure out what you want from it—your goal—and that will drive you and your strategy.

Why do you need a goal and a strategy?

Promoting a film is tons of work and the only thing that will keep you doing that work, which is absolutely exhausting, is a clear reason to do so—a goal. The only way you are going to achieve that goal or have a chance at it is with strategy. If you have no goal, you are not going to do all the heavy lifting that's required to make it a success. You are going to skip doing social media, you are going to skip entering festivals that require too much work and you are going to give up with a few rejections.

Further, if you don't know what your goal is you will not know what strategy to use to achieve what you want and that will frustrate you.

Figure out first and foremost why you made your film.

For example, I'm a screenwriter who made a film (vs. the director who usually makes the film—more on that in *Chapter 10*). I wanted to get interest in my feature screenplay—*Lunch Ladies*—a surreal, quirky comedy/horror with two middle-aged female leads, but the industry would often tell me there was no market.

I got sick of hearing that nonsense, so I decided I would save my money and make a proof-of-concept short based on the feature to show the powers that be that there were plenty of people who would pay to see *Lunch Ladies*—and they should fund it.

Every step of the process after the short was in the can was with this goal in mind:

1. *Email every blogger and magazine I could find that wrote about horror/cult film to get them to review it—why? Maybe some producer out there would read about* Lunch Ladies *and want to make it.*

2. *Prove* Lunch Ladies *has a market all over the world and money can be made (this is more drivel the industry loves to spout—that comedy doesn't play overseas)—as many fests as I could all over the world.*

3. *Have a great IMDb page[1]—Put up photos, film fest release dates, reviews, awards, key words, special thanks, etc. I figured anyone wanting to finance my feature would first go to my IMDb page to check out the short.*

4. *Make a website—Show industry folks how I would market the film because unless they see the potential, they won't get it (I had a school store, hairnet club, fan art page, geography lesson, announcements and more).*

5. *Build a fan base—Get busy on social media so I can find my target audience (it becomes crystal clear who that is when you see who follows you) and fans. If I know my target audience, I know who to market it to. If a producer knows there is a fan base and who they are, that helps to get it made.*

6. *BE SEEN! It had to be seen. Not sit on my hard drive. It must play everywhere it could no matter how small or how big—because someone may see it and help.*

---

1 IMDb—Internet Movie Database—this is explained in more depth in *Chapter 2.*

The goal of getting a feature made influenced all my choices in the festival run and gave me a strategy. I wanted to make the feature so bad that it kept me focused and excited, even when I was exhausted and didn't want to work. I would come home from my day job, write blogs for my website (each took about two hours and I wrote over 200 over the course of the film), post on Facebook, Instagram, Twitter, populate my Pinterest page, write reviewers, talk to fans, talk to other filmmakers, see other filmmakers' films, do interviews, and generally bop 'til I dropped.

I am certain a huge part of *Lunch Ladies'* success on the circuit was because of what I did above. The film is great (remember, you gotta love your film), but there are lots of great films. It's the work I did that took it to the next level.

Have I achieved my goal of getting the feature made? Not yet, but I'm still trying and having a great ride—who knows what the future brings and when it will happen or if it opens the door to something else?

Why did you make your film and what is your goal?

GET A FLIPPING GOAL!

CHAPTER 2

BE PREPARED

(press kits, websites, social media and being a goody-two-shoes)

I admit it.

I was the goody-two-shoes who always had her book report done a week before. Sometimes two weeks before. Okay fine! Three weeks. I'm not a procrastinator so it has always been easy for me to do things ahead of time—you have it harder if you aren't a goody-two-shoes, but it's a must for your sanity on the circuit.

Press kits, your website, IMDb page, social media handles, promotional pieces . . . you wanna have that stuff done BEFORE you start your festival run. Not while you're MAKING your movie, (don't get all crazy), but when you finish the film.

Why? Stop arguing with me; I'm trying to help you.

The reason why, hardhead, is because you are gonna be so busy promoting, getting into festivals and being a world traveler that you won't have time to do anything else. If you don't have time, then all the stuff you procrastinated on that you coulda done before the run is gonna be sloppy—which is why most press kits I see look like a four-year-old kid and their dog did them. Those filmmakers waited until the festival or publication asked them for a press kit and they either did one of two things:

1. *They had a nervous breakdown at the thought of adding more work on top of their crazy festival schedule*

and never handed one in (missing a huge promotional opportunity).

2. *They took a shot of tequila and made their press kit in a three-hour panic.*

That's not for you.

Press kits with typos, out of focus photos, bad layout . . . not for you. Missing a chance to promote your film because you haven't completed work you coulda done earlier? Nope, not for you. Having a nervous breakdown because you're overloaded with work when you're supposed to be charming and witty on the festival run? Nope, not for you.

You aren't gonna do anything amateur because if you do— no matter how good your film is—you are promoting that YOU are an amateur. You aren't.

And always remember, keep your goal in mind. If your goal is to get drunk at film festivals, take your clothes off and flip off the establishment, then hey, you don't need to have an IMDb page (you may need a sexy outfit though). Choose what you have to tackle (I had to tackle them all) based on how it furthers your goal.

BRANDING

What is branding? It's how you market your product (your film) and make it distinctive. You don't have to have your brand fully developed, but it's super smart to have an idea of what it is so you get off to the right start and don't have to backtrack.

There's a ton of stuff that can go into branding, but I just take it to the simplest level:

What is the essence of your film?

Now bottle it.

Lunch Ladies *is rebellious, bloody, yet full of heart, playful, loud, and takes place in a jacked high school. Therefore, those specifics became my brand.*

For example, I designed the *Lunch Ladies* website with a high school motif. The cast and crew are listed under ROLL CALL, reviews are listed under GRADES, there's a SCHOOL STORE and a STUDY HALL with teasers to watch. The writing is in -your-face, liberal, fun, and can be offensive—like the film.

Once you have a concept, stick with it and your ideas will evolve into a specific, identifiable look which captures the heart of the film. Be consistent—use the same fonts, colors, logos, and writing style and you'll be golden!

IMDB

IMDb, for those of you who aren't addicted to reading banal information about movies and movie stars, is the "Internet Movie Database." You want your short listed on IMDb because it's the go-to place that people look for information about a film. It's going to move your short up in the search on the Internet, and it's going to give it legitimacy.

I started my IMDb page immediately after the film wrapped— well before it was edited—because my cast and crew worked so hard, for so little, the least I could do was get their credit up—who knows what jobs it could help them land? Get people's credits up as soon as possible. After that's accomplished, add to your page as much as you can, as often as you can. Get a poster up. Get a trailer up. Get your *"special thanks"* up, get photos up, get your synopsis up. Put them up NOW (later on, you will spend so much time adding reviews, wins, festivals, etc. you won't have time).

Your IMDb page will be the place you visit constantly throughout your film's life by keeping it up-to-date. The initial process of getting all the names and credits correct takes work, so do it now; you won't have time later, and your cast and crew are gonna be irked if they've waited a year and you don't have their credits up.[1] Not cool.

Yes, Grasshopper, IMDb is a beast.

You will be so frustrated from the learning curve (wait until you have to tackle posting your wins) you'll swear your head off, scream, wallow in self-pity, cry and send nasty emails to some employee at IMDb who will ignore you. It's super confusing. In fact, you may need a Ph.D. to figure it out. Keep at it like I did, and you will learn to tame the beast that is IMDb.

When you get the hang of it, you'll love it. Nothing is more gratifying than adding new information about your film and seeing it show up for the world to see.

In addition, once you really get going, the IMDb people begin to know your short. They probably hate you because you're constantly updating and making work for them, but who cares you're a self-centered filmmaker—the point is, eventually, instead of it taking two weeks for information to be approved and go up, it will take two days because the powers that be know you are filling the page with real information (not lying and padding it). They will get your updates up ASAP.

PRESS KITS

I'm not gonna sugarcoat it. Press kits (or EPK's—Electronic Press Kits for those in the know) are no fun to make and it takes a while to get them right. You have to have patience. But, that's why you are doing your press kit NOW, right?

---

1   Email every single person on your cast and crew and ask them to send you their direct IMDb link (unless this is their first credit). If you've got "John Smith" on your crew and you link it to the wrong profile because there's thirty "John Smith" profiles, it's a nightmare change. Trust me, I hooked up profiles to the wrong people at first. Learn from my excruciating time-wasting experience.

Don't be overwhelmed. I know there's a ton of ideas on how to make a press kit and that can freak you out. It did me. But, listen, just pick a template that speaks to you. Or make up your own style. No one cares. There are no press kit police. All that people care about is how it's organized, how it looks and what it says. There's no right or wrong way. Be creative, be smart, make it look good, represent your film.

My press kit took about a month to complete. Choose people you trust to edit it; they'll find the mistakes you miss. Push your ego aside, get feedback and listen. Think of it as a job resume; make it as perfect as you can.[2]

I decided not to list my reviews (although you may want to) because I have so many and I didn't want to be constantly updating it, but I will sometimes attach the best ones when I send the kit out—depending on who is looking at it.

Also, the length of your kit is dependent on you—mine was long because I had so many in my cast and crew—also, I like to talk a lot (if you haven't noticed.)

If you wanna check out my press kit, go to lunchladiesmovie.com/contact and click the download link. I think it's pretty good. If you don't like it, jeez. What are you, the press kit police?

SOCIAL MEDIA HANDLES

If you don't despise social media, then wow—you are ahead of the game. Most everyone hates some type of social media—and you have to have them all (Instagram, Twitter, Facebook, Pinterest, YouTube, Vimeo, etc.), so stop whining like a baby. Nothing is going to get in the way of your goal. Especially, not something as banal as social media.

---

[2] If you have 120 people in the cast and crew like I did, you're going to misspell a ton of names; and that's disrespectful to those that helped make your dream come to life. Get everyone's name right, check them over and over before you send it out.

The key to social media is, and I'll talk about this more in depth later, you must find a way to love it. Social media is the kingpin of all your promotion. Love it like unicorns, puppies, and rainbows.

Take it a little at a time. You don't need to have a huge following right away; you don't even need to start posting until the film is on its run. You don't need to do all the social media channels at once. You can build them a little at a time. But get started. Open the accounts, create your handles, populate your photos—because once you are on the circuit you will need to promote, and you won't have time to set it up.[3]

For your handles, try to remain consistent so people can easily find your film.

If your Facebook is the same as your Instagram, you only have to tell people one handle, and that's easy to remember. Some people only have Facebook. Some only Instagram. Some both. You need all types of social media to really promote or you will miss opportunities, so make the handles as uniform as possible.

Purchase your domain (address) for your website first (if you decide to make one), then base all your handles on the site's name. If you do it the other way around, you may find that the handles you've set up are not available for your site.

> **Important—make sure your website name is fifteen characters or less:**

For my domain I chose LunchLadiesMovie.com, because my first choice of *LunchLadies.com* was taken. In retrospect I should've chosen *LunchLadiesFilm.com* because Twitter only allows fifteen characters.

---

3   Handles are the way people find your film on various social media.

Therefore:

@LunchLadiesMovie is the handle for all my social media except for Twitter which is **@LunchLadiesFilm**—Learn from my screw-ups.

WEBSITE

My website is my favorittttteeee promotional tool and I highly suggest making one and starting it now as it takes a while to get it up and running.

It took about a month learning curve to figure out how to build it, but it has been invaluable. A website will be your go-to spot to send people—it has your social media, your blogs (if you blog), your announcements, your trailer, your cast, crew, and synopsis.

Everything is there in one beautiful place.

Start with picking a great domain (fifteen characters or less, remember?). There are many companies you can purchase it from, but I recommend Wix.com because it's a one-stop shop. You can use their templates to build a website (for free!) then purchase the domain and hosting from them at the same time—easy.[4]

For those of you who have never made a website (like I hadn't) and don't understand the difference between "hosting" and "domain" (like I didn't)—think of it like real estate:

- *The website is your house.*
- *The domain is its address.*
- *The hosting is the land it sits on.*

---

[4] If possible, make the website yourself. It will save you tons of money because you will constantly need to make updates to your site. If you don't learn how to do it, you will always be paying someone to make these simple changes for you and waiting around for them to do it.

HOW TO PICK A DOMAIN

You will want your first choice, but often that's already been bought by someone else so you may have to settle like I did, remember? I wanted LunchLadies.com and ended up with LunchLadiesMovie.com.

Once you've got a domain you're happy with, it's time to build your website. I had no clue what company to pick (there are many out there that allow you to use their premade templates), but Wix had great reviews and was cheap, so I took a chance.

Good call. I pretty much love it. The support is super helpful and the site I created from their template looks legit. Pay for your hosting and off you go!

If you're really strapped for cash, you can opt for Wix's free hosting. However, with the free service, they print **Wix** on the headers and footers. It looks super amateur, so I say cough up the cash and pay for the hosting.

Of course, if you're already choking from the aftermath of your overinflated film budget, then okay, go for the freebie— some site is better than no site!

PROMOTIONAL ITEMS

The two things you want to have before your festival run are your postcards and business cards. If you're strapped for cash, opt for the postcards. Eventually, you will want both because they are useful for different reasons.

Postcards are super important because that's what you will use to promote your short at festivals. Hate to be the bearer of bad news, but most audiences aren't going to seek your film out—I know it's awesome but there's a lot of awesome films. Folks attend fests to support friends, see certain genres or something specific and your baby probably isn't even on their radar.

You will get on their radar by having postcards displayed (most fests have a table where filmmakers can put their cards) and handing them out. People do pick up cards from the table and see films that interest them, and many will see your movie just from you handing them a card and introducing yourself.

I highly suggest printing postcards no bigger than 3X5. I had a larger size and though they were really cool looking, they were a huge pain. They didn't fit in my purse, they didn't fit in my pocket and I'm sure people would pick them up and be annoyed at how flipping large they were and leave them in the bathroom after peeing.

Print your image on one side of the postcard and the back will have two columns. One column will be blank, this is where you will put your labels (discussed in *Chapter 7*) and/or addresses if you end up mailing them to specific people.

The other column will have your concise logline, your website (if you have one) and YOUR INFORMATION ON HOW TO REACH YOU. I know this is a major DUH, but I have seen postcards with nothing but the name of the film and the logline.

I envision some three-piece suit picking it up and saying:

"This film is genius! I must invest five million in the sequel . . . ummm . . . who do I call? Forget it, I'll invest in that condo instead!"

Business cards are needed primarily for when you meet industry people.

Sure, you can give them a postcard, but it shouldn't have personal info on it—they sit on festival tables for the world to see and you don't want some stalker calling you on your cell phone. You do, however, want Guillermo del Toro calling you on your cell phone– so you will want a business card WITH personal information on it for Guillermo.

Business cards are also great for a night on the town when

you don't want to carry bulky postcards or brazenly promote your film. You will meet someone new, possibly someone hot, trade cards and they will say "Oh, wow, you made a movie? What's it about? Can I buy you another cocktail?" EVERYONE you meet is a chance for promotion, and of course, a hot date.

Have your cards professionally done. I know it's tempting to save money, but don't print them yourself on that dot-matrix printer hooked up to your ancient Commodore VIC-20.

Cheap cards just make you and your film look cheap. Plus, there's a certain pride in having a nice-looking business card; it feels good passing them out and gives you a boost of confidence.

It's perfectly fine to wait until you are in your first festival before printing anything, but it's best to have the artwork ready to go because it will take time to get it right. This goes for posters as well, which you will want once you start the run. Printing is the least of it; you can do a rush if needed, but rushing artwork is always a bad idea.

More promotional items that you can start thinking about include pins, pencils, stickers and other types of swag. It's not necessary to have swag, but I do think it gives the film a push and pays for itself in the end. I had some fun things when I started and added more during the run.

CHAPTER 3

SPREADSHEETS FOR SUCCESS

(get organized—prevent screw-ups)

I'm going to teach you to set up some super organized spreadsheets which will maximize your money and chances at success on the circuit.

It's not glamorous, but it will prevent screw-ups.

Disclaimer—If you are as anal as me, then you have permission to skip ahead whenever it gets boring. But for the rest of you delinquents, pay attention.

THE FILM FESTIVAL GRID

First, open an Excel Spreadsheet or scribble in a three-ring spiral notebook if you're a Luddite. Excel will be easiest as you will want to sort columns, but if you don't have the program, that's okay too. Having any list will be a huge help.

Title it:

FILM FESTIVAL DATES

Why do you need this spreadsheet?

You need it so you can keep track of all the rules and dates to enter.

Every film fest has a ton of rules and entry dates and they are all different. You will have to read all those boring rules and keep them straight because you don't wanna waste money entering your film in a festival where it can't be accepted.

They'll still take your money. They'll just disqualify you.

With a Film Festival Grid, you can easily track everything, so no mistakes are made—your early bird submission dates (cheapest time to enter), which festivals need premieres, which coincide, what length of film is accepted and more.[1]

Your fest run will probably last a year and a half if you are doing great. It can last longer, but my feeling is to get out, don't overstay your welcome. Go into distribution when your time is up and don't hang around like a twenty-two-year-old dude hanging around high school stalking hot freshmen.[2]

If you ascribe to this way of thinking (and if you don't that's okay, you can be a creepy old dude stalking hot freshmen—seriously, no judgments), insert sheets on your spreadsheet for two years, one for this year, one for next. Because this year you won't make the due dates to enter some festivals and will have to enter next year.

To recap your pages on your spreadsheets are:

1. *This Year*

2. *Next Year*

If you're into overkill like me, add one more page called:

3. *At A Glance*

This will be where you can easily see which festivals you got

---

[1] Some festivals require premieres. There are several types of premieres—World Premiere, National Premiere, International Premiere, Regional Premiere and who knows what else. The first time your film plays, that's its World Premiere—that will also be either your National or International Premiere depending on where it plays. Then there are regional premieres—festivals that will only demand that you haven't screened in their city before. Premieres are a pain.

[2] Of course, if some hot freshman wants to date you, who are you to say "no?" So sure, be in fests if they pursue you (vs. you pursuing them). That's not overstaying your welcome—you're hot, what can you say?

in and which you didn't. Here you will add all festivals you enter in one column, and in the other two columns, you will pull from that list which festivals you got in and which you didn't. Only do this IF you are nerdy like me and like to know your percentage of success and failure or which festivals you have entered "At A Glance."

Here's what your spreadsheet tabs should look like:

"This Year" will be the festivals you will enter this year.
"Next Year" will be the festivals you will enter next year. Duh.
Now it's time to organize both sheets exactly the same.

1. Title the first column—FILM FESTS

Here you will list the name of the festival, what platform you submitted it on (platforms will be discussed in *Chapter 5*) and when the festival notifies filmmakers of acceptance—this will help you when festivals are rude and don't have the courtesy to tell you your film wasn't accepted. If the due date has passed and you never heard from them, you can be certain they want you to get lost. It's good to know when to get lost and stop dreaming you got in their festival.

2. Title the second column—INTERNATIONAL

This is where you make sure the festival takes international entries if it's outside your country. Sometimes you will be so excited to enter your film and you forget to read the rules and you pay and then realize they don't take international films. They will never refund your money, trust me. Basically, this is an idiot reminder to make sure you check.

3. Title the third column—OSCAR

Only a handful of festivals are Oscar-qualifying. If you win one, you can be in the running to get nominated (there are other ways to qualify but this is the simplest). This helps with decision making when/if you are low on cash. If you really want an Oscar, you can check that column to see which ones are Oscar-qualifiers and can weigh their cost against the others that aren't.

4. Title the fourth column—LOCATION

This is important because some film festivals require premieres and premieres are always based on location so you need to keep track of what area of the world you submit to.

For example, most festivals in Austin, Texas are notorious for requiring a premiere. If you decide you wanna be in Austin Film Fest, wait to enter SXSW (which you will also know is in Austin because you put the location in your spreadsheet) because if you get in Austin, you can't be in SXSW anyhow. Nothing is more aggravating than paying $50 to enter SXSW, getting in Austin, then getting in SXSW and realizing you flushed $50 down the toilet because they won't let you screen because you already screened in Austin.

More information on premieres is in *Chapter 4.*

5. Title the fifth column—WEBSITE

You want the festival's website here so you can click it up easily. It will save you time in the long run as you will want to check their website many times if you get in—or see who was accepted if you don't get in.

6. *The next six columns (six through eleven) will be the entry dates and fees of the festivals—title the columns respectively: EARLY BIRD, EARLY BIRD FEE, REGULAR, REGULAR FEE, FINAL, FINAL FEE*

This will help you strategize your money. You can obviously sort your spreadsheet many different ways depending on what you need. One way you will sort it is by EARLY BIRD ENTRY DATES. These are the dates you want to enter by and will keep you on your toes to never miss a deadline.

The reason you list the fees (even though admittedly it's time-consuming to do this) is so you can easily keep track of the money you are spending, and you can weigh whether you want to wait to enter at a later date if you don't have the cash at the moment.

Sometimes early bird entry fees are not that much cheaper than regular fees, sometimes they are similar, sometimes they are drastically different. If you know the consequences of not entering a festival by a certain time, you will be much more likely to make better decisions with your money.

Then, once a week like clockwork, sort your spreadsheet by early bird entry date and submit to the ones that are due. You will never miss an early bird entry that way.

7. *Title the twelfth column—FESTIVAL BEGIN*

This is important so you know which festivals coincide in case you get in two that run at the same time. This happens a lot. You can check the dates so you can wisely choose which festival you will attend. That way you won't annoy the programmer by gushing that you are going then backing out when you realize there's another fest you'd prefer.

8. *Title the thirteenth column—FESTIVAL END*

It's good to know the length of the festival. As mentioned,

sometimes you get in festivals that coincide, but sometimes one lasts three days while the other is twelve so you can actually go to both.

Why don't you put the festival beginning and ending all in one column such as April 15-19 like I did the first time? Because then you can't sort the columns separately, which you may need to. Learn from my screw-ups.

9. *Title the fourteenth column—LENGTH*

This is how long the film can be for acceptance into the festival. If your short is fifteen minutes and the festival only takes films up to ten, you cannot enter. But they will still take your money and disqualify you. See a pattern? Once again, if they get your money it's THEIRS FOREVER.

If you find out the festival is not a fit, I suggest still keeping it on your spreadsheet and greying it out. You will enter so many festivals you will forget which ones you researched and you will waste time unless it's on your spreadsheet:

"I almost forgot Blah Blah Fest! Why didn't I enter Blah Blah Fest? Blah Blah fest is awesome! Let me look up the rules . . . oh . . . that's right, I tried to enter Blah Blah Fest two months ago, but it only takes films that are blah blah, I wish I had remembered, now I just wasted ten minutes researching Blah Blah Fest a second time."

10. *Title the fifteenth column—PREMIERE STATUS*

Do they require a premiere? You may even want to consider having a separate spreadsheet for premieres to keep things in line because this can get confusing fast.

11. *Title the sixteenth column—NOTES*

This is for anything else—like "hey, this festival pays for a hotel if I'm accepted," or "hey, this festival doesn't give awards, forget it, I need awards," or "this one needs English subtitles to submit" or "they only take films made in the last eighteen months."

If you are a good little rule-follower, your spreadsheet will look something like this:

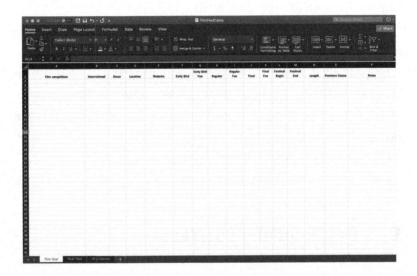

Excellent job! You have your Film Festival Grid set up.

But wait, you aren't done, you also need to make one more spreadsheet . . .

THE VIEWING GRID

This is where you will list every single person outside festivals that you send the film.

It will come in handy time and again.

Put anyone you sent your short to here—industry people, social media folks you've met, reviewers, press . . . their handles, their emails, the dates you sent them your film, where they are from, notes on who they are.

Create it NOW.

You will need it when you want to ask people to vote for the film if it is up for an award, or to spread the word when you get distribution—you now have a cultivated list of people to ask for help—complete with emails.

You will also need it if you can't remember who someone is down the line and they are gushing to you—you can look on your Viewing Grid and KNOW who they are.

Lastly, you will need it when you make the feature as there will be so many who will tell you during the run that they want to be part of it when it happens. You may not be able to hire them, oftentimes we don't have a say when a film gets produced, but you will have their names and how to reach them if you DO have a say.

The Viewing Grid is incredibly useful!

Now that you've made these really boring spreadsheets that are super useful . . .

LET'S ENTER SOME FESTIVALS!

Wait, what's that you say?

> **You don't have a clue what festivals to enter?**

Except for . . . please, no, please don't say it, I said don't say it! Don't say . . .

Sundance!

Ugh, Sundance. I mean okay whatever, Sundance fine, enter Sundance, Sundance, but listen, Sundance—quit saying SUNDANCE!

There's a whole world of incredible, terrific festivals out there that aren't Sundance that are just waiting for your film, so let's play . . .

CHAPTER 4

WHICH FESTIVAL SHOULD I ENTER?

(a game of ups, downs, thrills, and chills)

Entering festivals is a game. The ups, the downs, the excitement when you win, the disappointment when you don't . . . it's an emotional, heart-wrenching, exciting journey full of hope and fear.

The most important thing you can do to win the game (other than having a great film and rolling the dice) is play smart.

Which is why you have your Film Festival Grid, right? No mistakes for you that cost you money or make you look stupid to judges because you didn't follow some rule.

The second part of playing smart is choosing the right festivals to enter.

But where do you start?

There are literally thousands.

First, ask yourself if your film has more than one genre it fits in or if it has a niche.

If your film is a drama, obviously you're not going to enter it in horror festivals, and you've saved yourself tons of money. However, if it's a drama that has elements of the fantastic, there are horror/fantastic festivals you could enter—that opens up a world of possibilities. In fact, you may find your film actually does better in the realm of horror/fantastic than mainstream fests.

This may seem simple, but I know of filmmakers that didn't even know their film had elements of terror, so they never entered their movie in horror festivals. And because their film was so dark, they had a hard time getting in mainstream fests. Therefore, their percentage of acceptance was low and they believed their film wasn't any good. But the real problem was, they marketed it to the wrong types of festivals.

I nearly did the same.

Lunch Ladies is a comedy/horror. At first, I thought it fit more on the mainstream circuit because it's not scary. I decided I would enter very few horror festivals. When it won its first horror festival (Best Comedy/Horror—**Nightmares Film Festival**), I realized I needed to enter as many horror festivals as I could.[1] *Lunch Ladies* got in fifty percent horror and fifty percent mainstream. Imagine if I'd only entered mainstream!

Think about if you have a niche as well—maybe your film is female-led, or LGBT, or deals with science or food, or is extremely short. There are festivals that cater specifically to areas like this and more, so you want to make sure you enter any that may be unique to your film's subject matter or production.

Next, research festivals to see the types of films they like by googling them, looking over their websites and talking to filmmakers.

Filmmakers are the best source because most have very opinionated viewpoints on which festivals are lousy, which ones aren't, and which ones may like your film.[2] They may even be

---

1 Nightmares (nightmaresfest.com) is a great festival in Ohio run by Jason Tostevin. This was the first horror fest *Lunch Ladies* got in and the first award we won for Best Comedy/Horror. Jason creates an incredibly supportive atmosphere, and it's a ton of fun.

2 Check out Facebook groups, writer groups and networking events to find and talk to filmmakers. You can also look at last year's film fest's programming; contact filmmakers whose film played and ask them how the festival was or what they recommend. Most filmmakers are super cool and happy to share advice.

willing to go to the programmer and recommend your short if they like it—I've had this happen. Your colleagues are a wealth of information and support.

You can also look on **Film Freeway** (discussed in *Chapter 5*) to see the best-reviewed festivals for ideas—however, that can be inaccurate—most filmmakers will say the festival was great even it wasn't in fear of retaliation—maybe the fest won't take their next project if they say how they really feel! Of course, if the festival has bad reviews you know it's really awful because enough filmmakers were willing to speak out even if it could hurt their chances of ever being in the festival again.

Screenwriting and filmmaking magazines and film websites also often do stories about the best film fests for your money. These are good research tools as well, but they miss a ton of amazing film fests to review and often shout-out the same ones over and over. But these, coupled with research from above, will give you a good idea of where to start.

Another way to focus your list is by Oscar-qualified festivals.

If you don't care about winning an Oscar, then who cares about zoning in on entering Oscar festivals.[3] Remember, WHAT IS YOUR GOAL? But, if you do wanna win an Oscar, then enter every Oscar festival you can. The Academy updates a list every year—*Oscars.org*—and this is where you can find which festivals to enter.

Soon you will be able to narrow down a preliminary list, which will get longer and longer throughout the run as you hear about more opportunities.

No one can make this list for you. Sure, you can be lazy and

---

[3] If your film wins Best Short at an Oscar-qualifying Festival, you are now in the running for an Oscar. In the narrative short film category, about one hundred fifty films qualify every year (there is also an animation shorts category as well). Ten make the Oscar shortlist, then five get nominated. There are other ways to qualify for an Oscar as well, and you can find the rules on the Academy's website.

copy some other filmmaker's list who is willing to give it to you, but what's right for their film is not necessarily right for yours. You will still have to research every festival they chose to make sure it fits, and there may not be any on there that fit your niche—only theirs.

Your own focused personal list gives your film the best possible chance to succeed. You spent so much energy and love on your film, why wouldn't you give that same amount of love and energy into making sure it's being submitted to the right places?

FEEL-GOOD FAKER FESTS

The majority of festivals are legit but there are a few skanky ones out there. I call them "Feel-Good Fakers." Feel-Good Fakers could care less about films or filmmakers and are in the business of making money. They do this by caressing egos with pop-up red carpets (anyone can set up a red carpet, is it a real event?), tons of feel-good awards and fees for things that should be free. They have no legitimacy.

Before entering a fest, do your due diligence. Check their website and social media, see who is behind the event, do they have an actual screening of the film, do you have to pay for awards or trophies?[4] Reelport, a film festival platform (I will explain platforms in depth in the next chapter), does this work for you.

However, not all platforms do background checks like Reelport and you will need to be on several platforms to submit

---

4   There are some festivals that only have online screenings that are legit; but my feeling is, why pay to enter a fest that is online only? When your fest run is over, you can easily get your film online yourself—either your short will get distribution, or you can put it up on YouTube or Vimeo. What you want is theatrical screenings—screenings in a theater are not easy to do yourself because it's expensive.

to all the fests you want. It's up to you to research every fest and use your instincts—if it seems like a Feel-Good Faker, it probably is!

DOES THE PREMIERE MATTER?

There's a ton of scary rhetoric out there about what will happen if you don't premiere at the right festival; it's like you will contract some rare disease like Pellagra (thank you Lenny Bruce) if you make the wrong choice.

People agonize over what festivals they should enter and accept because of it.

I bought into this fear for about four seconds, and then decided . . .

I'm gonna premiere with whoever wants me first.

I'm sure there is SOME strategy of holding off to premiere at a prestigious festival to kick off your short, but . . .

I haven't seen any research proving it matters.

I hear talk. I hear advice. I read stories.

Yet, I never see any concrete evidence that your short is hurt if it premieres at the "wrong" place.

In fact, I see great films premiere at top tier festivals and go NOWHERE. I see films premiere at not so great festivals and go SOMEWHERE. And vice versa. Further, is it the festival that gives prestige to the film? Or is it the film that gives prestige to the festival? Maybe the success of the film is really because it's a great film not because it premiered at Berlinale.

Please, someone, give me some facts instead of scare tactics!

Since I don't have FACTS, I will go with my gut.

I believe if you have a great film IT DOESN'T MATTER.

Lunch Ladies did not premiere at one of the top ten festivals in the world and still it screened at over one hundred festivals including some of the best on the planet, won a slew of awards, got an amazing sales rep, distribution all over the world, loads of press and I was able to turn my back on the idea that the premiere mattered.[5]

I'm just sayin' . . .

Don't stress yourself about it.

Trust you will premiere in the right festival for the life of the film.

---

[5]   *Lunch Ladies* premiered at HollyShorts.

CHAPTER 5

ENTERING FESTS AROUND THE WORLD

(how to think big)

I have always thought big. It's shocking to me when people don't, because thinking big means you believe you have something big to give to the world, and doesn't everyone have something big to give to the world? No matter how small? I believe we all do.

Think big!

Anyhow, I'm a dreamer, I think big. So, when I told some haters I was going to enter *Lunch Ladies* in festivals all over the world, they laughed.

"*WTF? The* Lunch Ladies *abroad? Clarissa, c'mon.*"

It's true. *Lunch Ladies* is as American as it comes—it's about two murdering high school *Lunch Ladies* in love with Johnny Depp. Doesn't get more American than that. In fact, Mexico doesn't even have *Lunch Ladies* or a WORD for *Lunch Ladies*—there's no such thing as a Lunch Lady and many countries are the same.[1]

---

[1] The international premiere for *Lunch Ladies* was **Mórbido Festival** in Mexico City and the film has screened many times in Mexico—including **Feratum International Fantastic Festival**, **Post Mortem Festival** (where the film won second place—Honorable Mention Red) **Festival De Cine Y Comedia**, **Kino Muestra** and **Stuff MX**.

But remember my goal? To prove my comedy/horror film could play all over the world? So even though I felt a little crazy and scared (I don't like to fail either and I could definitely fail) and frankly a little egotistical (how dare I think *Lunch Ladies* can play outside the USA?) I decided I wouldn't listen to the haters and enter it in foreign festivals. Besides, I love meeting people from different cultures, and I knew I wasn't gonna meet them if I didn't enter the film in festivals outside my home.

Most Americans don't know jack about entering film festivals outside the USA and I was no exception. I had to do a lot of research, trial and error (lucky you, you just have to read this book) to figure out how to do it.

Let's start with platforms, and I don't mean the shoes. Though I do love a nice platform.

PLATFORMS

A platform is a site that a film festival contracts with to collect films for their viewing.

In the old days, and there are still many festivals that operate this way, especially in Europe, you would have to submit your film directly to the festival. If you wanted to enter you would have to send them a DVD of the film, a cast and crew list, synopsis, photos, and a fee if one was due. It takes a lot of time to send all this material to each and every festival.

One day, someone got smart and started film fest platforms.

On a platform, you upload all your materials ONCE. You find the festival you want to enter, pay the fee to the platform—who in turn takes a percentage and gives the rest to the festival—and then you hit SEND. That's it.

Huge time saver as you can enter thousands of festivals in a snap.

The platform I use most is **Film Freeway** because it's incredibly user-friendly and is where the majority of American and a good amount of foreign festivals can be entered. However, there is more to life than Film Freeway—not all fests can be found there.

For example, world-famous **Clermont-Ferrand International Short Film Festival** ONLY uses **Short Film Depot**—if you want to enter Clermont-Ferrand (and trust me you do, it's incredible)—the only way you can is through **Short Film Depot**. Other festivals only use **Festhome** or **IAMAFILM**, while some fests are listed everywhere.

Reelport (which has been around since 2004) was started as a project supported by the EU to reduce waste (no more DVDs sent to fests, everything done online) and to connect filmmakers to festivals in Europe and around the world.

Reelport has fewer fests to enter than many of the other platforms, but, as mentioned in *Chapter 4*, each fest has been vetted. They research everything from how old the festival is, to website and social media channels, venues, who screens submissions and more—therefore every fest listed is legitimate. If a mistake is made and one is found to be fake, they refund all submission fees to the filmmaker and ban the festival from the site.

BONUS SIDENOTE—*Reelport has gifted a first-time user discount for readers of my book! Like most platforms, they charge a service fee (two euros) for festivals with no submission fee. They are waiving this for YOU! 100% off! They are also giving a one-time user code of 20% off any submission. Wow! Check the footnote for instructions.*[2]

---

[2] Valid for first-time users of Reelport—go to reelport.com, sign up and search for fests you want to enter. Before checking out, email Reelport at **support@ reelport.com**, mention the name of this book and which free fests you are entering—Reelport will give you codes to waive the processing fee. For future use, every free festival has a different waiver code associated with it, so anytime you enter one just email Reelport for the unique codes. For your one-time user code of 20% off festivals with a fee—enter this at check out: **1b5c4438-fffc-4c0e-aa28-4f8e80e026b6**

You need to be on as many platforms as you can handle.
I was on six:

- *FESTHOME*—festhome.com
- *FILM FEST PLATFORM*[3]—filmfestplatform.com
- *FILM FREEWAY*—filmfreeway.com
- *IAMA FILM*—iamafilm.com
- *REELPORT*—reelport.com
- *SHORT FILM DEPOT*—shortfilmdepot.com

Other platforms exist, and they come and go (most recently WithoutABox run by IMDb closed its doors)—three that are popular, but I never joined simply because the six I was using were enough for me are:

- *CLICK FOR FESTIVALS*—clickforfestivals.com
- *FESTAGENT*—festagent.com
- *FILMFESTIVALLIFE*—filmfestivallife.com

You may find you like those, your choice, you don't always have to do what I do, jeez.

In addition, there are still festivals across the world that don't use a platform at all. You have to submit directly to their site like the old days. The entries are almost always free, and it's sometimes difficult to figure out when submissions open, what they want and how to do it. Further, sometimes it's not in your language. But Google Translate it because I'm telling you, some of the best festivals in the world don't use a platform.

Some of my favorite ones that the film got in that I had to submit through their site were:

- **Bucheon International Fantastic Fest**—*South Korea*—
  bifan.kr/eng

---

[3] This made sense for my film; but may not for yours as this platform is only for French Festivals. You will find which countries "get" your film. The French like *Lunch Ladies*—it got programmed a lot in France. Therefore, it made sense for me to be on a French Platform to submit to festivals in France that could not be accessed by any other platforms.

- **Fano International Film Festival**—*Italy*—
  fanofilmfestival.it
- **Filmets Badalona**—*Barcelona*—festivalfilmets.cat/en
- **Hell de Janeiro**—*Brazil*—helldejaneirofestival.com.br
- **TromaDance Film Festival**—*NYC*—
  www.tromadance.com

Once you are set up on the platforms, you can easily start filling out your Film Fest Grid by reading the rules and due dates of festivals you want to enter. The fests that are not listed on a platform, you will have to go to their websites and find information there.

Festivals that speak your native tongue are easy to submit to, but if you decide to go for the gold (ones around the world) there are a few things you need to know.

SUBTITLES

You will need at the very least, English subtitles. Even if your film is in English you need English subtitles. Why? It's often easier to understand a foreign language by reading than hearing. Programmers may speak English, but they probably read it even better, hence, English subtitles.

I know what you're thinking, oh, no, that's money to get subtitles!

It is an expense, but English subtitles are relatively cheap (it cost me nine dollars a minute) and once you have them it actually pays for itself because tons of foreign festivals are free to enter vs. American festivals which are seldom free and can cost twenty to fifty a pop.

You only have to get in a few foreign festivals to break even with the cost of subtitles.

The cost of subtitles is based on how difficult it is to get the language translated. For example, English and Spanish are relatively cheap because they are commonly spoken in America. Martian? That'll cost ya. But still, for me, even the more expensive ones paid for themselves by the time the run was over.[4]

The company I use to create my subtitles is Captionmax—they are great, super helpful and very professional. Check the footnote for a special 15% percent discount coupon on your first purchase![5] Don't say I never did anything for ya.

Captionmax did three translations for me: English, German and Spanish. Every festival I got in other than those did the subtitles for free.[6]

There are two types of subtitles—Burned-in and SRT/VTT export files. Burned-in subtitles are part of the film itself. SRT/VTT are standalone sidecar text files which can easily be added to your Vimeo file for submission to the festival.[7]

What is a standalone sidecar text file?

You know when you are watching a video and it has a little toggle in the corner "cc" and you can pick the language you want to see it in? That's a sidecar text file. The filmmaker has attached the text file to the video (with Vimeo it's super simple) and now the viewer can toggle the "cc" on or off and choose from any subtitles the film has.

Nearly every festival will request SRT/VTT and they are cheaper than burned-in subtitles. They will probably be the only type you buy. Captionmax gives you both SRT/VTT together for one price but I mainly used the SRT.

---

4   German was the most expensive, but *Lunch Ladies* got distribution in Germany on Amazon's Prime Video and further two of the fests it got in—**Landshut** and **20minmax** gave me travel stipends to attend.

5   For 15% off the first time you use Captionmax—go to captionmax.com and mention the promo code: **CJacobsonFestBk19**. It expires within one year of this book's publication—so get it soon!

6   Generous festivals made the following subtitles for *Lunch Ladies* gratis: Catalan, French, Greek, Korean, Italian, Portuguese (Brazil), Portuguese (Portugal), and Ukrainian.

7   In the case of **Short Film Depot**, there's a spot to upload the subtitles separately as well.

Only once did I have to pay for burned-in subtitles. It's not common, and many festivals that want burned-in will do it for free for you if you have your SRT/VTT files or what's called a Dialogue List—which I'll talk about soon.

BURNING IN SUBTITLES YOURSELF

For the one festival that did require burned-in subtitles—I paid to have it done by Captionmax. There are online programs and apps that you could invest in that may make it cheaper than hiring a company. However, there IS a learning curve. Do you have time for it? I didn't. I also did not know enough about the different types of film files to be clear on what was compatible for screening—as I'm not a techie.

There are some platforms which require a burned-in film with subtitles. This was something I did tackle. The French site **FilmFest Platform** did not have a way to add a Vimeo link (which allows you to attach subtitles). You had to upload the short with the subtitles burned into the film. I decided to do it myself because it was only for programmers to view on a computer, so I wasn't worried about screening problems.

The app I used to burn in French subtitles (by using the SRT file I already had made) was called **Subtitle Burner**, and I got it on iTunes for $4.99.

It served my purpose and was way cheaper, but I never used it in any other way than for festival entry. More power to you if you figure out how to do it for a festival and trust the file will work to screen in the theater vs. just to be seen on a computer screen.

DIALOGUE LIST

A Dialogue List is used by the festival who will make you free subtitles. It lists the exact lines in the script to the action on the screen.

You don't need to invest in a Dialogue List until it's requested, as you may be able to get away with sending SRT files for a while. Some festivals will make them for you with just that. But eventually, if you are getting in enough foreign festivals, you will need it.

You will also need a Dialogue List for your sales rep to market the film to distributors—if you get a sales rep. So, it is a good investment, but it's not something you need right away if you are short on cash.

You COULD do this yourself, but it's not easy and you don't want to screw up, because if you do, your subtitles aren't going to match the picture. Let a professional do it, it cost me only six dollars a minute to have it done correctly. I used it over and over and it ended up paying for itself, as every festival that was able to do the subtitles for free with the Dialogue List, saved me hundreds of dollars.

On the following page is an example of the first page of *Lunch Ladies* that I had done by Captionmax.

PROOFREADING YOUR SUBTITLES

I don't know about you, but I cringe when I see subtitles that are misspelled.

Take the time to proofread your English subtitles and Dialogue List for misspellings and/or errors. You don't have much control over it in other languages (unless you are bilingual), so you must let go and trust—but you do have control over making sure the festival at least has a correct English file to base it on.

BONUS SIDENOTE—*After your foreign festival screening is done (don't be annoying, wait a few weeks as they are BUSY cleaning up from the craziness), ask the programmer if you may have the subtitles they made for your film. It will save you money*

		[MUSIC]
0:00:07	TITLE	Melvinville, CA
0:00:34	ON-SCREEN TEXT (on envelope)	Melvin High School 999 Cedar St Melvinville, Ca 94865
0:00:35	SERETTA	It came. It came! Okay.
0:00:39	LOUANNE (OS)	Open it.
0:00:39	SERETTA	Oh…
0:00:39	LOUANNE (OS)	Careful, Rett, careful.
0:00:40	SERETTA	Oh. Oh. Oh. "Dear Seretta…
0:00:48	ON-SCREEN TEXT (on letter)	Melvin High School 999 Cedar St Melvinville, Ca 94865 Dear Seretta and LouAnne: I am pleased to inform you that your Cheesy Burger Bites recipe is the Grand Prize Winner of Cook for Kids Charity. As a restaurateur and lover of the culinary arts. I am thrilled to be part of this amazing event. No child should
0:00:49	SERETTA (ON/OS)	…and LouAnne, "I am pleased to inform you that your Cheesy…
0:00:57	ON-SCREEN TEXT (on letter)	that your Cheesy Burger Bites
0:00:57	SERETTA (ON/OS)	…Burger Bites recipe is the grand prize winner…"
0:01:02	LOUANNE	What?
0:01:03	SERETTA	(screaming) (laughing) Oh!
0:01:08	LOUANNE (ON/OS)	"As a restaurateur and lover of the culinary arts, I am thrilled to be a part of this amazing event."

as you will want them for distribution purposes. Further, you will be a hero if you get in another festival in that country as you will save them time by having the subtitles already. Only ONCE did a festival refuse to give me subtitles.

SUBMITTING

Every week check your foreign platforms for new festivals to enter. Submit to all the free ones you can—why not? What have you got to lose?

If you are consistent, you will discover gems you never knew existed.

I found tons of great festivals this way. Also, take a look at the foreign ones that have a fee, often it's ten dollars or less vs. American festivals which tend to be around thirty.

In general, festivals in America, Australia, Canada, and the United Kingdom can be pricey to enter. Inexpensive or free entries will usually be in France, Germany, Mexico, Spain, Latin America, South America and Western and Eastern Europe. Italy is often free but sometimes charges as well. Read the rules closely to make sure your film fits.

Most platforms also charge a small processing fee (around two dollars) to submit to any festival.[8] Check their pricing deals. If you intend to enter a lot of festivals on Festhome, for example, buy a yearly pass. You will come out ahead.[9]

BONUS SIDENOTE—*A fun thing to do is make yourself a map on* amcharts.com. *Check off the countries the film screens in.*[10] *It can drive your excitement to enter exotic and remote places!*

WAIVERS

A waiver is a discount code that allows you to enter a festival for free. It's totally unfair to the people who have to pay, but it rocks if you score one. Only three times in the whole run did I ever ask for a waiver and these were from fests that the cinematographer on *Lunch Ladies*—Chris Ekstein—had a long track record with and hooked up for me.

---

8   Reelport has waived this for first-time users just for reading my book! Check footnote 2 for details.

9   Film Freeway has a monthly membership called "Gold," which may make sense for you as well. Short Film Depot has ticket books—you get a better deal on pricing, the more you buy in bulk.

10   I made a "Geography Lesson" on LunchLadiesMovie.com (see how I slipped in that promotion for my film—check out my website!). For every country and U.S. state the film got in, I would update the map, teaching ignorant Americans like myself where stuff was.

Other than that, I didn't ask because I don't think it's fair. Most festivals that charge fees do it to stay in business—they aren't just pocketing the cash.[11] Further, why should I get to enter a festival for free and ride on the backs of everyone else who had to pay?

There are exceptions, however.

About six months into the run, film festivals came to me and offered me waivers. If a programmer comes to you asking you to submit, it's only natural they should pick up the fee. I also think it's okay if you're an alumnus like Chris was (however, I don't blame a festival for turning down alumni) and, of course, if you are from a foreign country that has low exchange rates and/or can't send money through traditional means.

Others feel differently about waivers and say one should always ask for them as they can save you a lot of cash. There are also those that believe if you aren't entering on a waiver, the festival won't give your film any weight.

I haven't seen proof of it with *Lunch Ladies*.

We got in more than ninety-five percent of our film fests <u>without</u> waivers. We were offered five waivers to festivals we got in, five waivers to fests we didn't get in and there were loads that just reached out and auto-programmed the film after hearing about it on the circuit or seeing it at other festivals.

Asking for waivers is a personal choice; everyone has a different take on it, so do what makes you feel comfortable.

COVER LETTERS

A few platforms will allow you to send a cover letter with your submission.

Always have a cover letter. Some film festivals won't read

---

11 The reason some festivals (mostly abroad) don't have to charge entry fees is because their government supports the arts and subsidizes it.

them. However, I know several programmers in particular that look at them closely. It may not make a difference if your film isn't in the running for their festival. But let's say it's between yours and another. They're going to go with the film that took the time to write a nice cover letter.

In your cover letter make sure to mention if you have anyone in your cast/crew that is from the state or country the festival is in. Also talk about wins, reviews, or anything else positive and try to make it personal. Just don't come off like a bragging, narcissistic jerk. Be real, authentic, excited and proud.

This goes without saying, but never put down your film. I know that sounds like duh, but when I started writing cover letters, I would say insecure things like *"It's not for everyone, but I hope you like it."* Horrible! Makes you really wanna see it, right? After getting some great advice, I changed that to *"I know you're gonna love it!"*

Set up a positive viewing expectation vs. negative.

And if they don't love it? Ignore!

FOLLOWING UP

After every submission, send a short, to the point, email to the festival that your film is on its way and to watch for it. That's it. It just puts your film on their radar. No need to say how terrific it is or follow up again. Just ONCE and only ONCE do you reach out—right after you submit—*"hey, watch for my film!"*[12]

Also, for points, take it one step further when emailing foreign festivals.

Write them in their language.

---

12 Don't be the obnoxious person asking the fest every other day if they saw your film. Yes, they saw it, but now they don't wanna program it because you are annoying—see upcoming flowchart.

Google Translate and apologize for Google translating if you have to, but make the effort.

The fact you even tried is stellar. Wouldn't it be annoying if you spoke French and everyone constantly sent you emails in English? It's so entitled. Don't be the self-involved English speaker who makes everyone always read English.

HOW TO BE POPULAR

Every single time you get into a festival, win an award or get a review you need to update it on your platform page. I know you already have a ton of stuff you need to keep current—social media, your website, IMDb, press kit[13] . . . OMG quit whining, just do it!

Some programmers may not care that you've got an updated platform page. But there are those that do; there are those that actually look.

How do they decide between two equally great films?

Flip a coin? Talk to a therapist? Make a complicated flowchart?

---

[13] Luckily, you did your press kit ahead of time, so you've uploaded it to your platforms. I would hazard a guess that most filmmakers don't even have one up because they procrastinated. Now, they're so busy they can't do one at all—see how smart you are?

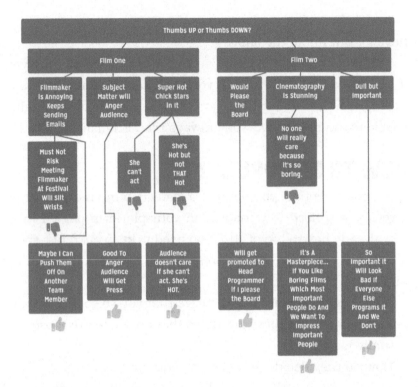

Who knows? But I do know you want any leg up you can get. A platform page that makes you look like you have some buzz is sure to be more enticing to a programmer than one that looks sad, lonely and depressed.

Remember, everyone wants to be associated with the popular kid.

Look popular, keep your page updated.[14]

---

14 FilmQuest (filmquestfest.com), a great festival in Utah I loved attending, said they look at everything on the platform when deciding which films to accept, not just the film.

44

CHAPTER 6

REJECTIONS RULE

(how to give zero cares about being rejected)

Rejections suck . . . until they don't.

Perhaps you aren't as naive as I was; after all, this was my first film, and I knew I had a great short (remember, love your film). I did not expect a ton of rejections—a few maybe—but only from morons with no taste.

I was that confident *Lunch Ladies* would get in EVERY SINGLE FESTIVAL.

When *Lunch Ladies* got rejected from the very first one I entered, I was shocked and confused. I'd seen some of the mediocrity they programmed—there must be a mistake. I immediately deduced that they didn't even view it—after all, I entered it one week before submissions closed.[1]

I knew it! They took my money and didn't even see it!

CREEPS!

This must be the only possible conclusion.

When *Lunch Ladies* got accepted into the second festival, this confirmed my ire toward the first festival. But then . . . the

---

[1]   *Lunch Ladies* had just been completed. In this case, entering late and paying more was an exception to the rule of always entering in early bird. I didn't want to wait a whole year to be in the festival and also this festival only allowed the film to be a year old (by next year I would be risking that it be too old to enter). However, once you get going, the majority of the time you should shoot for early bird.

film got rejected from the third and fourth festivals, then the sixth and seventh![2]

That's when I started to spiral . . . what if I really had a piece of crap on my hands and that first festival actually saw it and CHOSE not to program it?

But I kept coming back to what I knew.

Did I love my film?

Yes.

Was it everything I wanted it to be?

Yes.

Did people I know and respect who would tell me the truth, love it?

Yes.

Therefore, I knew there was something else at work—more than whether my film was good or not, and I thought hard about my goal.

Was I going to let rejections stand in the way of what I wanted?

I knew I had to combat any negative feelings about rejections and nasty rhetoric (there's always some hater just dying to bludgeon your film[3]) or I would not succeed. I would get depressed, bitter and at the very worst, give up.

That's when I set out to learn how to give zero cares about rejections.

YOU WILL NOT GET IN EVERY FILM FESTIVAL

Let it go. Your film is going to get rejected.

I don't care how great it is; it will get rejected. Even the best

---

2   **Tulsa American Film Festival** (tulsamericanfilmfest.com) was the fifth I entered and the film was accepted—it's a wonderful hometown festival screening at the historic Circle Cinema. I had a blast!

3   Usually this is a person who has never made a film or done anything creative in their entire life. Or they are simply jealous and unhappy. Ignore!

films in the world get rejected. There are no hard and fast numbers about rejections, but I've heard that ten percent is the average acceptance rate.[4]

That means ninety percent of the time you will hear the word "NO." You're gonna get rejected a lot, and if you're doing better than ten percent acceptance, you are the rarity. If you're doing less? There're all kinds of reasons for that too—and it's not always the quality of the film.

BONUS SIDENOTE—*I love telling other filmmakers which festivals* Lunch Ladies *didn't get in. It takes the power away from the "Nos," and if you have the courage to open up and admit your film didn't get in every fest to another filmmaker, they'll open up to you too. You will see and hear that everyone is being rejected. If you meet a filmmaker out there that feels superior to you because they got in a festival you didn't, they are a jerk— see Chapter 9 for more examples of jerk behavior.*

REASONS YOUR FILM IS REJECTED

Festivals program films based on what their audience wants, if it's a genre film, how long the film is, how many they can accept, what the subject matter is, if it plays well in their line up, and more.

Your odds go up for acceptance when you tick their boxes.

AUDIENCE

I was at a talk where some programmers at a prestigious festival (one of the top ten in the USA) were telling everyone to make documentaries because their audience will pay to see them.

---

4   I know you're dying to know. Fine—*Lunch Ladies* got in a little over thirty percent of the festivals I submitted to. There are films that got in more than *Lunch Ladies* and films that got in less, but you need to stop comparing— every film has its journey!

It went like this:

If all of us could just make a great doc, it'd have a high chance of being accepted vs. our narrative—they simply didn't get enough doc submissions and that's what their market was. I was super annoyed—it's not a valid suggestion. Making a documentary is a completely different skill than making a narrative!

However, I digress. The point being, their audience likes docs, so they program a ton of them. If you make a halfway decent one, you will probably get in.

Other festivals have no audience for docs, so the opposite is true—don't make a doc!

Some fests have conservative filmgoers, so they're not going to program your amazing *I Hate Republicans* film. Just the same, other fests have liberal filmgoers so they're not going to program your amazing *I Love Republicans* film. It will just anger their audience.

Festivals often think of the audience when programming the film.

GENRE FILMS

Is yours a genre film? If so, it'll be tougher for you to get into a mainstream festival. Why? Because it's mainstream. That means they can only program a certain number of horror films, for example. If they only have ten spots for horror, and they get one hundred amazing horror films, too bad. Ninety have to go. They have to fill the rest of the festival with dramas, comedies, and docs. That makes your odds go wayyyy down.

If you're submitting to a genre festival, on the other hand, and they get one hundred amazing horror films, they most likely can program every single one because that's the only type of film they're screening.

LENGTH

A film that is five minutes or less is probably going to get in more festivals than a film that is twenty minutes—**even if the longer film is superior**. Why? Programmers have hour-long blocks they have to fill. If your film is twenty minutes long, that means they have to turn down four five-minute films for yours, or two ten-minute films, or one five-minute film and one fifteen—you get the idea.[5]

It's like a puzzle; they are tasked with fitting in the most and best films possible into a time period. Sometimes they'd just rather program six films in a block than four—they get to reject fewer people that way.

Many will advise you to make a ten-minute film because the programmer can then easily fit you into a block. My advice is, make the film what it's supposed to be. Yes, you have to earn your time. Edit it until it squeaks (kill your darlings); have others you trust look at it, not just the editor, director, producer or writer. Get feedback. If it's a twenty-minute film, it's a twenty-minute film. If it's good, it will get programmed.

Sure, you may get in more festivals if your film is short, but no one tells you the upside of a longer film. Longer films have legs. That is, if you have a great long film, that's the one people are really talking about. It's the heavyweight in the program. It's more likely to be the one with substance and have more developed characters and story simply because there's more

---

5   *Lunch Ladies* was nineteen minutes. Early on, one genre festival wrote me a personal rejection email gushing that they loved the film, but they didn't program it because it was too long. The programmer suggested cutting it to fifteen minutes, because we would get in more festivals. We tried. It sucked. *Lunch Ladies* editor Amelia Allwarden is top-notch, and it was cut the way it was supposed to be. Later, I saw the films the festival programmed that were shorter than ours—several were not as good. In fact, we came up against a lot of these films time and again at other festivals we did get in and won in many competitions over them. It was not the quality of the film but the length that was the cause of the rejection.

time. Because of this, it's the one that has more chance to win prizes and maybe more chance at distribution.

The average Oscar-nominated short film is eighteen to twenty-three minutes long. Less than six percent are under ten minutes or less.[6] There's something to be said for a longer film even if you don't get in as many festivals as a shorter one.

They each have their place, but the point is, the length sometimes plays a role in whether the film is programmed or not.

ODDS

Sometimes, your film isn't accepted because they only have ten slots for shorts and the rest of the program is features. What are your odds?

Lunch Ladies was in a wonderful genre festival in Germany called **Fantasy Filmfest** (fantasyfilmfest.com). This was a very difficult festival to get into because they got three-thousand short film submissions and can choose only ten. The odds were tough. Win some, lose some—this was one we won.

Your chance at acceptance goes up or down with the odds each year of how many films are submitted to the festival. If the film isn't accepted, it doesn't necessarily mean they didn't like it. They could've loved it. There may have been a ton they wanted to program but only had room for a few.

On top of this, every single person in the programming department usually has to agree on the films selected. Imagine agreeing on films with your friends! Some of my favorite films in the world—other people I admire and respect, hate them. Every programmer has their favorites and often has to fight for them. Sometimes one film goes by the wayside because everyone can't agree.

---

6   Stephen Follows, "What do Oscar-winning short films have in common," stephenfollows.com (March 12, 2018)

What are the odds every programmer is gonna love your film?

SUBJECT MATTER

Maybe your film got rejected for the subject matter.

The festival got twenty amazing films about global warming. They can't take twenty films about global warming. Variety is the spice of life and their audience does not want to sit through twenty films about global warming. Maybe your film got nixed because this was the year everyone sent in films about global warming including you.

Or, maybe your film never got to the programmer, to begin with, because their preliminary judges passed on it. Your film is about dogs and they're all cat people. Meanwhile, the programmer is a dog person and would've loved it, but hey, she never got to see it.

Maybe your film is weird. *Lunch Ladies* is super weird. And there's a place for weird films. In fact, the French love weird films and *Lunch Ladies* plays a lot there and got distribution on Canal+. But other film festivals don't like weird films; they just don't.

DOES IT FIT?

They love your film!

But guess what, it's a dark comedy, and all the other comedies they've chosen are light-hearted. There's nowhere to program it that makes sense, so they reject it.

Your film must fit—it doesn't have to be the same subject, type, or even genre but it must screen well with the others they've chosen.

An example of this was when *Lunch Ladies* played at the wonderful **Filmets Festival** in Badalona, Barcelona. The block it screened in had animation, drama, comedy, and comedy/ horror. The programming (by Agusti Argelich) was genius, each short was so incredibly different yet fit together perfectly. He took the audience through highs then lows then highs again to end with the upbeat *Lunch Ladies*.

Try this out. If your film isn't accepted to a festival you are sure you should've gotten in, check out the films the festival chose; many times over the course of *Lunch Ladies'* run I would discover that the films screened would never play well with mine.

NATIONALITY

What nationality is your film?

This comes into play with international festivals. Programmers don't want to have fifty films from the USA and none from Getwerzistan.[7] It wouldn't be international.

What does this mean for you?

If there are only one hundred submissions from Getwerzistan and the programmers choose five, you've got a five percent chance if you're a Getwerzistanian filmmaker. If they have a thousand American films submitted and choose five, you've got a **point** five percent chance of getting in if you're an American. Wouldn't you rather be Getwerzistanian? Me too.

You are mostly in competition against the other films that are from your country.

This is why some film fests, in addition to having an international program, also have a national program. That way they don't have to lump their own country's submissions in with the international submissions. They know there will be more submissions from their home than anywhere in the world. They also want to support native filmmakers. The only way to assure that the majority of films programmed are from their own country is by adding a national program.

---

7   I love Getwerzistan. The mythical country of Getwerzistan gives all their money to the arts.

For an international festival, it's not just about the BEST film, it's about showing the variety of voices around the world and you can't do that if you only choose the BEST films. You must choose the BEST films from EACH country.

NEPOTISM, CRONYISM, FAVORITISM AND STARF*CKING

There are festivals which choose films simply because the filmmakers are alumni, simply because the filmmaker did some lab of theirs, simply because the film has an obnoxious pre-pubescent star of that stupid series in it . . .

Nepotism, cronyism, favoritism, and starf*cking on the circuit DOES exist.

But, it's no excuse to care.

Why?

Because it's a small equation.

In some festivals, it's a bigger equation, but most of the time you are not going to be rejected for those reasons. Further, even if a festival practices any of those tactics, it's only a small part of their programming, leaving room for all the outliers like you.

I did not know one person on the festival circuit, yet *Lunch Ladies* got in over one hundred festivals and won over thirty awards. *Lunch Ladies* also did not have one movie star in it. BOTH lead actresses won awards and got tons of amazing reviews.[8]

It can make you furious when you see a lesser film taking a spot from a better one just because they had an "in." But, at the same time, that's part of life.

---

8   Donna Pieroni, who played the lead, won Best Actress at **Crimson Screen Festival** in North Carolina, **Fano Festival** in Italy and **Women In Horror Festival** in Atlanta. Mary Manofsky, who played her right-hand gal, also won best actress at **Fano Fest**. Both women also received nominations from festivals including **Anatomy Crime in Horror**, **Austin Revolution**, **FilmQuest**, **NOLA Horror** and **Oregon Screamweek**.

In every facet of the work world, less-qualified folks get jobs because they know people. Less-qualified folks get jobs because they interned at the company. Less-qualified folks get jobs because their Daddy had money and donated to the firm's celebrity poker event.

Why should it be any different in the film world?

There is going to be unfairness no matter where you go.

What you must keep in mind is qualified films get in festivals all the time. Your film is qualified, it'll get in a festival. Stop worrying about what you don't have—connections—and start concentrating on what you do have—a great film!

Unless . . .

YOUR FILM ACTUALLY DOES SUCK

This is the one that messes with your mind the most.

Does my film actually suck?

I think you actually know the answer to this, deep in your heart.

I'm betting it's "NO."

But, let's just say your answer is "YES."

The sound is all jacked because you filmed right next to the airport, your lead actress was sleeping with the lead actor and he caught her cheating with the grip and they're supposed to be in love in the film but it's obvious they hate one another, you wrote the script in a drunken stupor one night and filmed the next day—who needs rewrites?

Okay, your film sucks.

Now that you know that, what do you do?

You give yourself a pat on the back and say to yourself:

"I made a film! Most people NEVER will do this even if they want to. It takes courage to make a film! I'll learn from this one and my next film will kill it!"

So, if your film sucks, whatever, you'll make another and it'll be great.

Last but not least . . . on why you shouldn't care about rejections—your rejection could be because . . .

THEY HAVE NO TASTE

It's one thing to go to a festival that your film was rejected from and see great films. It's another to go to a festival where every other film is lame.

That's when the lightbulb goes on in your brain: *"Hells bells, they have no taste!"*

There will always be programmers with no taste. They can be the most wonderful people in the world—they may even like some of the same movies you do, but deep down, you know it, I know it—they have no taste.

You, thankfully, have taste, so you just smile and know if your film had gotten in that particular festival it meant it was lame as well—that puts rejection in a whole new light.

Thank you, person who has no taste, for not choosing my film!

HOW TO HANDLE REJECTIONS

First thing to do is scream, yell, then send off a nasty email to the programmer who rejected your brilliant masterpiece:

"&*$# you! When I win my Oscar, everyone is gonna know that you're the *%#$*% film festival that rejected me! GO *&^$ YOURSELF!"

Ummmm. Nope. That's not what you should do.

EVER.

Surprisingly, however, film festival programmers take this abuse all the time. I can imagine their terror of even sending a rejection to a filmmaker. How will the filmmaker react? *"Are they gonna yell at me? Are they gonna grill me?"*

Put it in this light: A lot of festival programmers were or are currently filmmakers themselves. They care about filmmakers. They don't want to reject anyone. It's the worst part of their job. Rejecting people sucks.

To make it worse, they've probably seen three thousand or more short films. They only get to choose a program of thirty. They must reject ninety percent. Ugh.

Most likely, your film is being rejected for many reasons (as we just discussed) other than its quality—so, the rejections are not personal.

Then, say this mantra to yourself every day (even if you aren't a hippie like me):

"My film will get in the best film festivals for its life."

Trust that.

I trusted that and I had a heck of a ride! Getting rejected from Sundance had no bearing on that ride. Would I have gotten more buzz if *Lunch Ladies* got in Sundance? Sure . . . maybe. Who knows . . . but I do know that *Lunch Ladies* got a terrific sales rep and a distribution deal WITHOUT Sundance.[9] Therefore, did I need Sundance? No, I needed **Clermont-Ferrand**—that was the festival that made those successes possible.

OMG Clarissa! What is your beef with Sundance! My beef is, people think Sundance is the end-all-be-all. It's a great fest, but it ain't the only one, and there is too much energy lamenting over not being accepted to it.

If you start thinking that way, the rejections don't matter because it's giving no power to the festivals you don't get in and trusting in the ones you did.

When you get a rejection, respond:

"Thank you so much for watching my film, have a great festival!"

---

9   **Ouat Media**—ouatmedia.com

You will be surprised at what happens. You will feel more empowered than sending a nasty note. And, you may just get a wonderful reply back from the programmer—I've had several send me heartfelt thanks.

On a more practical un-hippie-ish note, if you respond to rejection like a jerk—they'll remember that. And you may just want to send them your next film. I have no hard and fast numbers on programmers accepting films after someone has been a jerk, but I pretty much bet they remember jerks and prefer not to program anything made by a jerk. FYI—it never pays to be a jerk.

I will tell you two interesting stories about rejections.

Lunch Ladies was in a top festival abroad. I had been talking a lot to the programmer and she told me, on the down-low, that the film was nominated for Best International Short. She told me not to tell anyone because the festival had decided not to announce nominations. Apparently, in the past, when they made nominations public, they got terrible emails from filmmakers that hadn't been nominated. So, in order to save themselves the headache of being yelled at, they simply didn't announce nominations.

Can you see how crazy this is?

The true win is getting selected for a festival. Getting nominated for an award is the icing on the cake. Yet, enough filmmakers in the past had their little feelings hurt about not getting nominated that they actually ruined it for the ones in the future that did—by sending nasty emails. Most films will never know if they got nominated at this festival– that's sad—it's a joy to know you were nominated!

Even worse than not knowing is you lose the opportunity for promotion—you can't publicize or post the nomination on

IMDb—all because a bunch of filmmakers in the past cried like babies.

Believe it or not, it happened a second time—another international fest told me *Lunch Ladies* was in the running for Best Short and not to tell anyone. So, you see? This is not an isolated incident or anomaly. It's happening a lot.

Be happy for other filmmakers when they get nominated for an award or get in a festival you don't—your turn will come. You'll get in something they won't, you'll win something they won't, there's room for all.

The other great rejection story happened at the Clermont-Ferrand Festival.

Lunch Ladies was short-listed in the competitive section but did not make the cut. However, the programmer told me the film was "very dear to his heart" and that they were preparing a series of programs around the theme of gastronomy for their fortieth edition. Would I be willing to screen it in that section instead?

Are you kidding?!

I was ecstatic and I thanked them profusely—*Lunch Ladies* was going to Clermont-Ferrand, one of the top short film festivals in the world! I didn't care what section it was screening in as long as it screened—what an amazing honor.

Flash forward to the festival . . . which was fantastic. I had a wonderful talk with one of the programmers at a party. He told me they were so relieved and happy that I hadn't been mad about screening out-of-competition.[10]

---

10 I'm not quite sure why people think being in the competitive section is EVERYTHING. I did run into some snobby filmmakers in the competitive section at Clermont-Ferrand that seemed to think they were superior to the films that weren't. They aren't! In fact, many of these "superior films" never got the type of distribution deals *Lunch Ladies* did.

I was shocked. I asked if they had other filmmakers who had been upset about this petty kind of stuff. Yes. They did.

WTF?

Instead of being thankful for a screening, other filmmakers in the past had been furious they weren't in the section they deemed more important—the competitive section!

Not me. I didn't care. A rose by any other name! *Lunch Ladies* screened just as much as any of the films in the competitive section. There was no difference in how many times it played. Further, I would bet that the audience liked the film even more where it was programmed—the *Tous Á Table* section—a section about food. The audience was prepped to laugh, and they loved it!

And guess what? The programmers also decided to put *Lunch Ladies* in the OPENING PROGRAM of the whole festival—one of only nine films out of hundreds—the auditorium seats over one thousand and was FULL. They further took *Lunch Ladies* to more festivals after Clermont-Ferrand ended, including **La Criée Tout Court** in Marseilles and **SESIFF** (Seoul International Extreme-Short Image & Film Festival).[11]

Question is, did they program the film in the opening program and at the other festivals only because it was a fit?

There were lots of films they could've chosen, why *Lunch Ladies*?

Or did they program it not only because it fit, but because I was thankful and not a pain in the neck? Who knows . . . but I'm sure being a pain in the neck always works against you.

---

[11] Clermont-Ferrand is such an important festival in France that several other festivals across the country screen some of Clermont's films in addition to their own choices. Clermont chooses the films that go.

CHAPTER 7

PROMOTION

(suck it up, you gotta promote)

This is the section where I tell you to quit kvetching that you *"aren't good at promotion and social media"* and tell you to suck it up.

Let's get one thing out of the way.

NO ONE likes to promote.

If you are the rarity that DOES, then good for you, you are way ahead of the game. But, for most of us, we'd rather cut our vein and bleed out than promote.

I was no exception; I hated it. It made me extremely uncomfortable and gave me anxiety. Yet I knew I could not achieve my goal without promotion. I had to do it if I wanted to succeed, and I had to learn to love it or I wouldn't do it.

Once I set out to love it, I wouldn't shut up about my film!

You will be the same.

The other hurdles I had to overcome were being overwhelmed and fear.

OVERWHELM

Promoting can be overwhelming as there's so much to do and share with social media. This can lead to being paralyzed and doing nothing.

The way I combatted this was to post something each day, no matter how small. Just be consistent and do SOMETHING, anything. You will see, it will snowball. Your baby steps will become a walk, then a run, and you will begin to get buzz about your project.

Once that happens, you will get excited and will promote even more.

FEAR

I feared people would think I was a narcissist if I talked about my film, feared people would not want to support me, feared people wouldn't care what I had to say, fear, fear, fear. I had so much fear and anxiety about promotion, I had to go to a therapist over it!

She told me some great things.

She said I did not know how people would feel about me promoting. I was putting my own insecurities on others expecting a negative reaction. These were my fears and that's all they were—fears. Not reality. If people didn't like what I was saying, they could unfriend or unfollow me. It probably had more to do with their own hang-ups than anything else.

The world changed after that.

Every time fear would visit me, I would fight it and force myself to be authentic and share what I was passionate about— my film.

I found out an amazing thing—my fears were unfounded.

I learned the majority of people are supportive. The majority of people want to be part of your journey. The majority of people want to hear about your success. The majority of people want to help you and WILL help you.

HOW TO START

People often ask me my "secret" for getting so much promotion for *Lunch Ladies*.[1]

It's simple, I took a pill and everyone wanted to talk *Lunch Ladies* 24/7.

ACT NOW—Send a check for only $199.99 to get your miracle bottle!

Sorry, I wish it was that easy.

All of *Lunch Ladies*' buzz happened because I WORKED hard. That's what it requires. So, roll up your sleeves!

TYPES OF PROMOTION

There are several ways you are going to promote. Through social media, through publications, blogs, at festivals, by promoting others and more.

SOCIAL MEDIA

Each of the main media channels—Facebook, Twitter, Instagram, and Pinterest—have different types of people following them. Sometimes there's overlap, but in order to reach the widest type of audience and meet the most bloggers and writers, you want to have all of them.

I met reviewers and fans on Twitter that I did not meet on any other channel. Same with Instagram and Facebook. Each one had people that did amazing things for *Lunch Ladies*—and many were only on that platform—if I had not been on Twitter, for example, I would not have met UK writer Ross Baxter, who

---

[1] *Lunch Ladies* got over eighty reviews/interviews, had a great fan base on social media, was covered on France's national news channel **France24** and several times on **Eerie Late Night Horror Channel** (eerielatenight.com) out of Pennsylvania.

made me GIFS and funny photos with the *Lunch Ladies* on it.[2] I used these extensively in promotion!

This is why I suggest you be on all of the sites, and you don't want to auto-share.

Auto-sharing is a handy tool that allows you to toggle a switch on the account and have it automatically post to your other accounts. It's easy. But it looks like jack.

A Facebook auto-share direct to Twitter just has a link of the post. It's boring. No one wants to click on the link because it's not visually interesting, so your Twitter feed, instead of being populated with photos, is filled with links to open the photos. No one cares, and no one is gonna follow that Twitter account except your cast, crew, family, and friends. You aren't doing all this work for them. You're doing it to find new fans, and garner interest from people who have nothing invested in your project.

An Instagram share to Facebook looks decent—this is the one you can often get away with—but you will still have to go into Facebook to correct issues.[3] All of the auto-shares have problems and the best way to avoid them is to post separate content on each.

I know it's a pain, but it'll pay off. If you can't handle the time it requires, then pick one channel and forget the others. Better to promote on one well, than to do all half-baked.

Now to the nitty-gritty.

---

2   Ross is an author of sci-fi and horror fiction. His varied work has been published in print and on Kindle. He stumbled on *Lunch Ladies* on Twitter, I sent him a link to the film, he loved it and the rest is history. He also represented the film by attending the **Misty Moon Festival** in London. We have never met in person—the amazing power of social media!

3   The problem occurs when you tag someone on Instagram. Let's say your lead actor has an account on Instagram @awesomelead—you tag them in the Instagram post, so they see that you've posted a photo about them. You share it to your Facebook and it shows up @awesomelead—which is weird in your post, because on Facebook their user name is @totallyawesomelead—so you have to go in and edit the post, deleting the Instagram tag and putting the correct one in

FACEBOOK

I used Facebook primarily for posting events, sharing reviews, interviews, fan shout-outs and supporting others who in turn supported me.

Whenever the film is in a festival, always create an event and tag the festival as co-host. This way if they accept co-hosting, it will show up on their page under their events. Most festivals will accept—I've only had a few who wouldn't. By doing this, you are getting a lot of promotion because anyone who goes to the festival Facebook page will see which films are playing in the events section. Yours will be there. Ninety percent of the other films won't because most filmmakers don't create events.

Further, by creating an event, it's specific about which venue the film is screening at, what time, and you can link to ticket purchasing as well. It's hard tracking down all this info (wait until you get to the festivals abroad and you can't figure out what's what) but you must do the legwork. You want people to see the film, right? Make it easy for them by delivering all the details.

Post on Facebook at least three times a week if not more. Be consistent and people will begin to take an interest.

INSTAGRAM

Instagram is my favorite. I had the largest following there. I really committed to posting and even hired a cheap company to help me follow people.[4] If you are posting regularly, talking to people on direct message, and responding to comments, you won't have time to follow accounts.

So, I do suggest a company to help you on Instagram. You will still have to work super hard, but they can take away the exhausting task of finding people to follow.

---

4   Just make sure whatever company you hire they don't pull the follow unfollow crap—which I think is a super lame move. Tell them you don't want to unfollow anyone that follows you.

What's all this "follow" stuff?

With most social media, the name of the game is following people. If you don't follow people you aren't going to have people follow you, and don't be a jerk and unfollow people once they follow you either (see footnote 4). No one cares if you have 10,000 followers and you are only following one hundred. It doesn't make you look popular (everyone loves me, and I only love a select few); it makes you look like a narcissist. Who cares how many you are following? Spread the love; as long as you aren't following more than are following you, you're golden.

Once again, be consistent; I posted every day without fail and set a daily alarm so I wouldn't forget. You have to be consistent to get momentum.

Connect with people. I responded to every comment, answered direct messages, and talked to fans. It takes time, but it's necessary. I can't tell you how often fans would post *Lunch Ladies* on their own Instagram page or story simply because we had a connection and they wanted to support me.

A word to the wise, however; be open, be kind, be supportive, but beware of energy vampires. They will blab day and night and get mad if you don't respond.

Until I learned to set boundaries, I had some major time sucks with energy vamps. Most people are great, but there will be some you have to put the kibosh on.

TWITTER

Twitter was the platform I dreaded the most, but once I got going, I loved it because the people are very kind and supportive on Twitter.

I built my base following horror fans. Figure out what your niche is, then start following those people. Eventually, someone will connect with you and post what are called "Follow Fridays." In this, they'll shout-out a few people and you'll all follow one another. Follow anyone you can, and that's how you will build your channel.

PINTEREST

For Pinterest, I made several boards, one promoting festivals, one with reviews, one with fan art, one with the film's trailers, and one that visually encapsulated the film. Because my film is about murdering *Lunch Ladies* in love with Johnny Depp, I posted photos of high schools, cheerleaders, Depp . . . anything that had to do with the *Lunch Ladies'* world.

I haven't had time to build the base, but I keep the page up and always promote it as it looks awesome. I use it to show industry folks what I want the feature to look like. Everything on Pinterest is visual, so it is almost like a director's handbook of how you envision the film.

YOUTUBE, VIMEO AND OTHER SOCIAL MEDIA

There are loads of different platforms out there, and you can choose whether you want to be on them or not. I have a YouTube and Vimeo account. The YouTube account looks good, so I promote that, the Vimeo I use mainly to host the film for festival submissions. I would've really loved to work on building followers for my YouTube account, but hey, there's only so many hours in the day and I simply couldn't keep up with it.

WHAT TO POST

Post film festival acceptances, reviews, red carpet photos, awards, and behind the scene shots of cast and crew.[5] But

---

5   Hopefully you had an "annoying" person on set who insisted on taking tons of photos. My lovely friend Bev Nero gave me the greatest gift ever by being "annoying." She showed up to set for support and spent the whole day snapping pics on her iPad. I had no idea the incredible present she gave me until I started promoting. She gave me at least 300 photos and more than fifty videos—she is the reason why I had such amazing content to post! If you haven't filmed your movie yet, make sure you have a Bev Nero on set.

think outside the box as well. You can share things that have to do with your film but are not your film.

Sometimes I'd find true crime stories in the news that I could post because they had an element of Lunch Lady crazy in them. Sometimes I'd find news about Johnny Depp I could use or humorous GIFS that fans made, like the *Lunch Ladies* on the cover of *Cosmopolitan Magazine*.

Craft your posts. Don't write the same old lines next to your photos all the time:

"We are so excited, it's festival number twenty-three for us!"

It gets boring. Don't ever be boring. Find an angle.

This was my angle: as mentioned in my section on "Fear," I feel self-conscious talking about my work. So, I used the characters in my film to help.

I wrote all my posts in the voice of the *Lunch Ladies* as if they were real people. The *Lunch Ladies* are murderers, but they have a good heart, they're underdogs, and they are rebellious. They will lie, cheat and manipulate to get ahead.

I'd get in a festival? I'd share a photo of the *Lunch Ladies* partying with a tagline:

"We robocalled Kerry Festival until they caved and programmed us! SUCKERS!"

It was actually fun. And it was different. By the end of the run, people actually thought of the *Lunch Ladies* as real people and if they commented or sent me a note, they'd address me, *"Hey Ladies."*

Whatever you do to make your posts interesting, make it yours, make it authentic and specific, make it content you'd want to read. Your campaign doesn't have to be wild or funny or serious or anything like mine; it just has to be something that shows some effort, that fits the film (its brand—*Chapter 2*) and is more than just *"Hey, I got in a festival!"*

BONUS SIDENOTE—*A major upside to being actively engaged and invested in your social media is you will discover your target audience. Age, type, men, women, kids, teens, gay, straight, blue-collar, white-collar . . . social media gives you a very clear and specific viewpoint on who will pay to see your piece because only those interested in the film will follow it. By the end of the run, I knew exactly who my audience was.*

REVIEWS AND INTERVIEWS

How do you get them?

Once again, by hard work—bloggers, reporters, and journalists are not going to just come to you to talk about your film. You can get a little mileage from festivals who have a strong base of press contacts, however, it is hard to get their attention (they can't review every single film at the fest). But, in more prestigious festivals, you are competing against films with PR reps who have an "in."

Further, your short may get a few reviews at a festival, but the buzz will die out soon if you don't keep it going.

It is up to you to get your film out there and get reviews.

BUILD A LIST

Make a list of the publications you want to contact.

Include the name of the editor/blogger, their website or social media handle and their email on your Viewing Grid (*Chapter 3*).

You don't need to make a list of three hundred folks right away—what are you, a glutton for punishment? Shoot for ten or twenty new entries a week—whatever you can handle.

HOW DO I FIND PUBLICATIONS TO SPEAK TO?

Google! What did we do before Google?

We used the Dewey Decimal System and it was a nightmare. So, yes, googling is a lot of work, but hey at least you don't have to cart yourself down to the library and use the Dewey Decimal System. Now THAT's work.

Lunch Ladies fit in the horror and cult genre, so I focused on that niche first and it paid off—I googled Horror Reviewers, Horror Bloggers, Cult Film Bloggers, Short Film Bloggers, Short Film Reviewers, Weird Film Reviews, Strange Film Reviews . . . and so on.

Another great way to find publications is by using social media—for example—I became part of Twitter's horror fan base by following horror fans. I saw reviews people retweeted and would, in turn, follow and contact the writers who wrote them. I got a lot of coverage of the film this way.

Further, because Twitter's analytics are so great, it caught on fast that I was in the horror community. Horror Reviewers began to show up in my feed of suggestions to follow.

You can also follow other short films that are getting reviewed and reach out to the same publications. Be a detective! Podcasts, YouTube shows, social media, hometown papers, word-of-mouth, look everywhere—make a goal to find a certain number a week to contact and don't stop until you reach it.

WHAT DO I PUT IN THE EMAIL?

Whenever possible, do not email your coveted contact *"To Whom It May Concern."*

Not only is it impersonal, but you sound like you have a stick up your a*s. Search the site for the editor's or reporter's names. Sometimes many different people write for a blog or site.[6] Find a specific person and email them, asking them to look at your

---

6   If you don't get a response from one writer at a site, you can work down the list and reach out to others. Sometimes one will talk to you whereas another won't.

piece (if there is no direct email, use the "Contact Form" on the site).

Tell them a little about the film and ask for what you want—a review, an interview, a spot on their podcast, a diamond tiara, whatever you think you can score. If you have awards you can mention those, as well as upcoming festivals, great reviews or unique things that may pique their interest—I had a lot of fan art, so I'd often include photos. I probably rambled on way too long; shorter is better, but you get the idea. End by thanking them and attach your press kit.

Make sure to follow up if you don't get a response. My rule was to bug the person three times max over several weeks (not over several hours—they will hate you). Often the third time I reached out I'd get a lovely response that they'd been swamped and meant to cover the film but hadn't had a chance. If I hadn't been persistent, I would have never gotten the review.

Keep diligent track of whom you have contacted in your Viewing Grid, when and how many times you've emailed them. Keep an accurate log of everything you do with the press, because you may want to reach out to them again with more news—you will need contacts, names, and history.

When *Lunch Ladies* got its first distribution deal in the USA on Amazon's Prime Video, I went to my Viewing Grid and was able to easily contact every single news outlet who had done initial coverage. I asked them to shout-out the news. Most did![7]

WHAT ARE MY ODDS OF GETTING A RESPONSE?

The majority of publications will not respond; that's why you need to add to your list with new people every week—it's a numbers game. Do not get discouraged if you get a "no" or your first thirty never reply. Just keep going.

---

[7] **Tennessee Horror News** (tnhorror.com) even designed a special Prime Video ad for me to promote with! Thanks guys!

Initiate contact and forget about the results. The results will take care of themselves. Sooner or later, someone will review your film.

By the time I was done with my festival run, I had reached out to more than two hundred different people.[8] Some were bloggers with ten followers, some were reviewers with 150K followers, it did not matter. Publicity is publicity and if your review is a good one, you can list it on your IMDb page, on your website and share it with your social media.

The key is to get as many people talking about your film as you can. Sure, it's awesome to have a site with a huge following do it, but that doesn't make it necessarily better than one that has a smaller following. You never know WHO is reading what. You could have a very tiny blog review your short and their dad happens to own an island in the Bahamas and decides to fund your feature. You never know.

Anyone who writes about your film, small or large, is helping you!

Be realistic as well.

Your flick is a pebble in an ocean of boulders, so expecting a heavyweight like *Variety* to do a story right off the bat when you have no buzz is naive. You are more likely to get smaller bloggers and independents at first and can build on it—one does lead to the other! Further, smaller reviewers are often more open to looking at new content, and there's less competition because less are querying them.

This is not to say you should not go for the 800-pound gorilla;

---

8   I have not stopped! Now that *Lunch Ladies* is in distribution, I continue to reach out to people to cover it. When will I hit my wall? When I no longer have passion about it being seen, something in my artistic world takes its place, or word-of-mouth has taken over.

I believe in always aiming high. Sometimes you hit a home run. Aim high for sure but be realistic.

Getting the first twenty or so reviews are the hardest, then it gets easier. People really do start to hear about your film, and you get more responses. The day will come when people reach out to YOU! For me, it took about three months of getting reviews and building buzz before I got an email in my box:

"Hey, I heard about Lunch Ladies, may I interview you?"

SHARING THE NEWS

I've heard many stories from publications taking the time to see a film, review it and post it—yet the filmmaker never shares the news. Being a writer, I know it's a ton of work to do all that they do. Crafting a good short blog would take me an hour or more plus time to post and promote.

They are doing all this for your film; most are not even getting paid for it.

To not share and shout-out the magazine, website or blogger that did that for you is super uncool. They have dreams just as you do, they want their work to be read and their site to get followers and advertisers; the least you can do is publicize the flipping review (unless it's a bad review—ignore!). Have respect for what they are doing, and they will be in your corner, help you and support you.

This goes for festivals as well. Follow all their social media. Like their posts, advertise the festival on your channels, share content, retweet, help them promote you by you promoting them—it's a symbiotic relationship.

I promoted the heck out of Clermont-Ferrand, and guess what? They, in turn, promoted the film the week of the festival on their Twitter, which has 11,000 followers—there were over four-hundred films screening—no way they could shout them all out—but they retweeted all _my_ posts about when and where _Lunch Ladies_ was screening.

FILM FESTIVALS

Ideally, you will attend as many festivals you can. More opportunities arise if you are actually there in person promoting the film. Obviously, you can't go to them all—it's cost prohibitive—but I'll cover below what to do about the ones you can't go to.

The point is, attend as many festivals as you can because they open doors to meeting fans, meeting people to collaborate with, meeting industry, meeting press, even meeting other programmers who can put you in other festivals![9]

Plus, they're loads of fun.

POSTCARDS

First thing you need to do is make LABELS to put on your postcards which have the date, time and location of the screening. This is important. Most people are not going to flip through a catalog to find out when your short plays unless they are filmmakers—and even they don't like to do it.

Make it easy for everyone; you want people to see the film, so have the details of the screening right on the postcard.[10]

Second thing to do is make a few labels which have the link to your film with the password. These are for industry folks you meet. If they don't have time to see the film at the fest, or miss it, they have a direct link without contacting you (which most won't take time to do).

---

[9] I met Agusti Argelich, Head Programmer of Filmets at Clermont-Ferrand Festival—if I hadn't gone to Clermont-Ferrand, I never would've met him. Filmets was one of my favorite festivals!

[10] Most festivals will have a designated table for filmmakers to leave their promotional materials. That's your first stop, drop twenty postcards there and swag if you have it. Then carry some with you for whenever you meet people.

If you're lucky, they'll watch your film in their hotel that night and sign you to a fifty-million-dollar deal because they're drunk and exhausted.

POSTERS

A lot of times filmmakers don't bring posters to a fest, and they are missing out on a huge promotional push for the film. I've been to festivals where there were one hundred fifty films playing and only twenty-five had posters. You put yourself at a disadvantage if you don't have one up because there will be people that will attend one screening and not another simply because they saw a poster.

This happened to me several times. Granted, I had a sick and twisted poster that some individuals (especially men under the age of thirty) said looked like lady parts, but regardless, I am certain that posters help get people in seats. For argument's sake, let's say it doesn't. You put up a poster and not one person comes to your screening. So what? You still got promotion. People will remember the name of the film or the visual of it if they saw your poster.

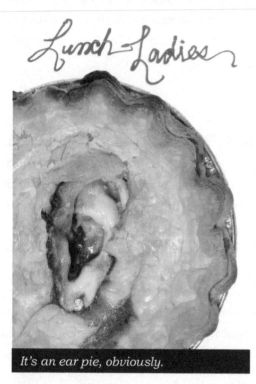

It's an ear pie, obviously.

This may seem like a little thing, but any advertising will help your short.

In addition to the poster, you will need a foldable easel. Some festivals allow you to tape your poster to the wall, but most will want you to provide an easel. You can buy easels from Amazon for under twenty dollars. Mine came in a box that is fifteen inches by two and a half and the easel folds out to sixty-three inches—see how compact they are?

I have two sizes of posters for the easel that are mounted on foam core—a large one for local festivals that I can shove in my car and tote over to the fest, and a small one for festivals I have to travel to that will fit in my suitcase or carry-on. Most printing companies can easily make the foam core posters for you in addition to the regular ones.

BUSINESS CARDS

As I discussed in *Chapter 2*, business cards can wait if you are short on cash, but you will eventually want to cough up the moola. They are super handy at festivals when you don't want to carry around a big postcard, and they are needed for industry folks as they will have personal info on them that you won't want on your postcard.

SWAG

This is not a must by any means; however, I found that swag is the gift that keeps on giving. Fans love it. It will show up on social media, at screenings, heck they'll wear it to the supermarket . . . I've even had swag appear at festivals *Lunch Ladies* wasn't even in!

I think the investment you make in it pays for itself many times over. When a fan talks about your film and promotes it, people listen. With swag, you've given them something to promote WITH.

Having swag is also a nice thing to do for the festival. They love it because they get to give their audience a perk. I've run into a few festivals that told me not to bring swag, but on the whole, it's met with excitement. Always ask.

WHAT TYPE OF SWAG?

Decide on something that is inexpensive, clever, and easy to mail. You will be sending a lot of swag to fans and to festivals that you don't attend.[11] It should be cheap, and by cheap, you also have to think about mailing. You want it to fit into a standard #10 envelope, so you don't pay more than the cost of a postage stamp.

Some great ideas:

1. *Stickers. SUPER CHEAP!*

   People love stickers, plus you can put them on everything you mail—you never know who will see your package outside who you've sent it to or what postal worker will

   handle it; it may be enough to make them look your film up online.

   Make sure you put your website on your sticker. Duh, right? Well . . . I made over one hundred stickers with no website. No way to reach me! Learn from my screw-ups. For my stickers I used a company called Print Runner—it was forty dollars for 2000 stickers—that's two cents apiece!

---

11 Anyone who does something nice for the film or is a fan, ask if they want swag. Chances are they do.

I had two sticker designs—one was my ketchup logo, the other was from a contest I ran on Instagram. The winner was Craig Mills of the UK who sent in the awesomely sick drawing entitled "Pair Nets" (see photo on facing page).

2. *Pins. SOMEWHAT PRICEY BUT WORTH IT.*

I used a shop on Etsy called MediasFrankenstein which I found to be the cheapest for a small run (seventy-five pins—about forty-seven cents apiece). They do a fantastic

job and guess what, there's a first-time user discount of 15% off just for you guys! Deets in the footnote below.[12]

Buying in bulk (500 pins or more) is the least expensive way to go and you can find companies that do that online, but I wanted two different pin designs and that meant buying in bulk twice. It fit my budget better to do small runs.

The reason why pins are worth it even if they are a little pricier is that people will WEAR them. And you will WEAR them, and people will ask you about the film because of it.

---

12 For 15% off the first time you use MediasFrankenstein—go to etsy.com/shop/MediasFrankenstein and enter the promo code during check out under "Redeem gift card or Etsy Credit": **JacobsonFFBook**

3. *Pens & Pencils. NO ONE THROWS SOMETHING*
   USEFUL AWAY.

   Pens & Pencils are always a good swag item because people won't throw something useful away. Even if someone
   hasn't SEEN your film, they'll take a pen or pencil from
   the promo table.
   Maybe later they'll
   look your short up
   or see it at another
   festival.

   I had pencils made
   that said: *"Property*
   Of Melvin High," as
   if the *Lunch Ladies*
   had stolen them. I
   bought those from
   a terrific company
   called The Ink Spot
   and people really
   got a kick out of them.[13] And guess what? If you go to the
   footnote below you can get 10% off your first purchase![14]

4. *Creativity rules.*

   Be creative. By far the favorite swag item I had was hairnets. I wrapped them in tissue and put a *Lunch Ladies*
   sticker on the back. They were one of the first things to

---

[13] The cost for five hundred pencils was twenty-six cents apiece. They were
   hard to mail individually so I seldom sent them to fans as they didn't fit in
   a #10 envelope too well, but I always brought them to festivals and mailed
   them in bulk to fests I couldn't attend.

[14] For 10% off the first time you use **The Ink Spot**—go to ink-spot.com and
   enter the following promo code during check out or mention it if ordering via
   their chat: **CJacobsonFestBk**

always go at festivals. Maybe people thought they were condoms, but whatever they grabbed them like hotcakes.

Once opened, several people took photos of themselves in the hairnets. This prompted me to create a *Lunch Ladies* Hairnet Club on my website. Folks even sent me pictures of their dogs and cats in hairnets. What incredible promotion!

Plus, hairnets were cheap and super easy to mail because they were flat. They came out to sixteen cents apiece!

Condom or hairnet, you decide!

EXPENSIVE SWAG

I maintain . . . go cheap!

However, there will come a time when you wish you had something special to give to a wonderful programmer who bends over backward to promote your film and/or treats you like gold.[15]

Sure, you can send a bottle of wine or cupcakes, which I've seen done. And yes, it's a very nice gesture—but frankly, it's pretty forgettable and doesn't take much effort or thought.

---

[15] Not to mention, you may want it for a mega fan who constantly promotes your film, or a giveaway on a podcast or a filmmaker who helps you score a screening . . . you just never know who you want to give something special and for what reason.

Further, it's not promoting your film in any way. Unless of course, your film is about wine or cupcakes.

Therefore, if you decide to have some items that are a little more high-end (and by high-end, I mean twenty dollars or less) for special occasions, go for something that has your logo, photo, or theme of your film.

T-shirts, mugs, flash drives, nice pens . . . these are all cool things that can easily be made ahead of time. Or you can be even more creative and come up with something crazy and unique.

For my film, I totally lucked out.

Rae Ganter, the owner of Twisted Wonderland Perfumery, started following the *Lunch Ladies* Instagram page.[16] Or maybe I followed her, I can't remember but who cares the love was there and I was amazed by her creations—handmade products with outlandish, wonderful horror themes:

Coffin soaps with Freddy, Jason, and Pennywise, body oils with scents like "Mistress of the Dark," "Enchantress," and "Silent Hill," delicious perfumes, morbid, fun and delightful lip

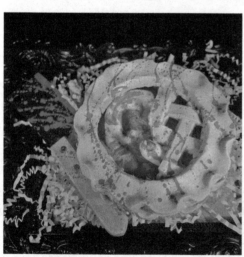 balms, linen mists and candles.

Yep, this Twisted Wonderland Perfumery insanity seemed the perfect partner to the even more insane *Lunch Ladies*. But . . . would she think I was nuts for asking if she'd be interested in making me some swag for the film?

16 twistedwonderlandperfumery.com—best stuff ever!

To my shock (this was in the beginning before I learned how supportive most people are to filmmakers) she was warm and wonderful, and the BEST that could happen, happened:

She not only loved the film, but she also created the sick and twisted "Lunch Is Served Pie Soap" complete with its own "delicious crust" and a bloody ear, then carried them on her website giving the film even more promotion![17]

IF YOU ARE UNABLE TO ATTEND THE FESTIVAL

The promotion doesn't stop.

Be in the loop about what's going on at the festival by keeping on top of their social media and following their pages. A few weeks before, send postcards with labels (and any swag you have) to them so they can put it out on their promo table.[18]

You may not be able to attend, but you will have a presence.

Why is it so important to have a presence?

Case in point:

I couldn't go to the **Santa Barbara Film Festival** until the last two days of their run, so I sent my postcards and swag to the programmer ahead of time. I knew there would be a lot of press there and I wanted to make sure they were aware the film was playing even if I wasn't there to network until the end of the week.

Because I did this, I had a distributor reach out to me. He was there at the beginning of the fest when I wasn't, had seen my postcard on the promo table, was intrigued, saw the film, liked it then called me to offer me a deal.

He told me very few filmmakers had postcards sitting out

---

[17] I am giving away the scoop on *Lunch Ladies*, but it's a spoof on *Sweeney Todd* so you can imagine how excited I was to give away such a clever piece of promo.

[18] With the exception a few foreign festivals (some are just too cost prohibitive or their customs are a nightmare) and a few others I sent postcards and swag to almost every single festival the film was in.

(even ones that went!). He said he knew ahead of time what he wanted to see based on the program but always took a look at the promo table to see if anything would pique his interest that he didn't have on his list. *Lunch Ladies* did. If I hadn't had a postcard out, he would've missed it.

LETTING OTHERS REP THE FILM

Is there an actor or crew member, fan or friend that lives near the festival that is willing to go for you if you can't? Several times I enlisted the help of others to be the face of *Lunch Ladies* when I couldn't—some even did the Q&A!

I'd first put out feelers to cast and crew, then if no one could go I reached out to friends and fans. I then got them a pass through the programmer (most fests are happy to hook this up for you), wrote up answers to possible questions that could be at the Q&A (if they were willing to do it) and sent them swag to pass out.

The following fests all had people there for me when I couldn't be there: **20minmax** in Germany, **A Night of Horror** in Australia, **Bentonville Film Fest** in Arkansas, **Crimson Screen Horror Fest** in North Carolina, **Hexploitation Fest** in Canada, **HorrorHound** in Indiana, **Knoxville Horror Fest**, **Misty Moon** in UK, **Oregon Screamweek** and **Twin Cities Film Fest**.

SENDING ITEMS TO THE FESTIVAL

A rule of thumb that I always follow is everything you do is a reflection of your film and the pride you take in it.

When you send your postcards and/or swag, consider not throwing a jumbled mess in a padded envelope then shipping it out.[19]

---

19 Sometimes the festival will even ask you to send a poster or you can ask if they would like one.

Think a little bit about the presentation.

Below is a photo of how I mail my stuff—the postcards were wrapped in butcher paper (a fun pun for murdering *Lunch Ladies*) and sealed with a *Lunch Ladies* sticker. I put the swag in wax paper sandwich bags (*Lunch Ladies* takes place at a high school during lunch—what says "school lunch" better than sandwich bags?) and I sealed those as well with a *Lunch Ladies* sticker (remember how handy I said stickers would be?).

These little things have an impact. Over the run, I had several programmers comment on how I shipped my items—they got a kick out of it. Sure, they were going to rip into the butcher paper and discard the sandwich bags, but they appreciated the detail.

There will be festivals that don't care how you wrap it. But, for the ones that do, they'll bend over backward to make sure it goes out on the promo table and they will know who you are, what your film is, and help you!

PRESS LISTS

This goes without saying, but if you get a press list from the festival, make sure you email every single one about your film asking them to see it or meet you. You'd be surprised how many filmmakers don't do this. They probably don't do it because it's a time suck, but it works. I got much press this way.

Try to think of a personal way to reach out to press other than, *"Hey, I saw that you will be at the festival, my film is too. Can we meet?"* Pretty dull, eh? They are getting tons of emails like this with no personality or passion. You want to be on their radar because you sound interesting and your film sounds interesting. Even if they don't have time to meet you, which most don't, they may reach out and ask for a link to see your film.

Be authentic to your voice, show your unique personality; you will get some bites that way. If you are full of fire like I am, it will turn some people off, but it will also get bites. You only need a few! Just don't be milk toast.

SIMPLE WAYS TO GET PROMO

Always include your social media, website, and teaser in your email signature.

Several times complete strangers that I had to email about everyday things would ask me about *Lunch Ladies* simply based on my signature. One time I needed a repair on a chair and reached out to the company to fix it. The person who responded not only fixed the chair but asked to see the film, loved it and in turn, became a fan who posted about it and followed all my social media.

Also, when people ask you about the film via email, all your information is right there in your signature. It's a time saver.

Always carry your postcards with you. You never know who

you will be in a conversation with. I can't tell you how many talks I had with Lyft drivers who checked out the film.

If you have artistic fans on social media who follow you—check out their pages when you have time. Twice I saw young artists on Instagram who posted—*"I don't know what to draw, what can I draw?"* Twice, I got great fan art that way.

WHAT ABOUT A PR PERSON?

When I started, I wanted a PR person right away. After some research, I discovered that my zeal needed to be taken down a notch.

The best rule of thumb is to let a PR person come to you vs. trying to find one. Sure, you can spend money right off the bat and hire someone, but most of us are not rolling in dough, and it would better serve you to spend that money later down the line when you have a little buzz and really need the help.

Save the cash or use it to attend film festivals.

Moreover, you're more likely to get a top PR company if they seek you out instead of the other way around. A good PR firm doesn't take every film, they take the ones they are passionate about. They are selective and really give catered attention to each film they choose.

I eventually took the jump in hiring a PR person when I was approached by *London Flair* at the **Palm Springs International Film Festival**.[20] *Lunch Ladies* had been on the circuit for eleven months. I had secured more than forty reviews at the time and had a lot of interest going. They reached out, asked to see the film and took it on.

I decided to hire them because I had been working about

---

20 *London Flair* (londonflairpr.com) is a top-notch firm out of London with offices in both the UK and USA. Their publicity work has been behind several Oscar-nominated and Oscar-winning Short Films. They are lovely people to work with and really care.

seven hours a day for eleven straight months promoting (in addition to a full-time job) and I was exhausted and needed help. I did not stop promoting the film one bit after *London Flair* took it on—I just could concentrate on other aspects of promotion vs. working so hard to find reviewers.

How did it work out with the PR company?

By the end of the run, I secured way more publicity for *Lunch Ladies* than they did. However, the exposure they got was different—it was for publications they had connections with that I could never have gotten, so it opened the film to a different group of readers/viewers. The marketing was also more focused on my work, which helped my career vs. just the film.

For me, having *London Flair* was the perfect timing (because of my exhaustion) and they were a perfect addition to my team (they balanced my promotional efforts by promoting the film in a different way). I loved working with them, and it was a joy.

But it would've been a huge mistake to start with them and skip doing any promotional work myself.

The people and connections I met were invaluable. They knew me and I knew them and that made it personal; so many reviewers shouted-out the film two and three times for me simply because we now had a connection. If you only have a PR person working for you and do no promo yourself, you will never have that personal connection.

Ultimately, no one cares about your film more than you. Connecting with people, talking about your film, no one will do it better than you. But, if you are lucky enough to have a great PR person to round out your team, and it makes sense, then go for it!

CHAPTER 8

ATTENDING THE
FESTIVAL

(expectations will kill ya)

Congratulations! Your film got in a festival and you're going to it!

You are going to have the time of your life!

You probably will, but you DEFINITELY will if you temper expectations.

I had tons of expectations when I started the festival run. Often, they were met. But sometimes they weren't. After some less than stellar things happened (check out my "SH*T HAPPENS" blog at the end of this chapter as one example) I knew I had to get rid of all expectations or end up being a bitter, victimized, "poor me" filmmaker.

Those types are no fun.

Since I'm a huge proponent of being fun, I made it a mantra to go to festivals for the adventure and to always remember that no matter what insanity occurred, *Lunch Ladies* was screening on the big screen with an audience. Wow!

Mostly, attending festivals have been some of the best times of my life.

But anything goes—some will be incredible and treat you like a million dollars while others don't care if you even show up—make the most out of your experience and look for the silver lining.

In fact, I've found that some of the "worst" festivals I went to actually did more for my film than some of the ones that were fantastic.

For example, I went to one festival that only cared about celebrities (at one event, in particular, that really annoyed me —filmmakers were not allowed to sit in a certain section which was roped off for their "celebs"), it was super expensive and worst of all I found out the festival was pocketing money on hotel rooms by up-charging filmmakers.

How sleazy!

However, this festival also had tons of journalists.

Lunch Ladies got so much advertising there, it was insane!

That was my silver lining. Who cares if they were creeps? The promotion I got was invaluable. Thank you, creepy festival, you rock!

Also, I truly believe MOST festivals want to do right. Sometimes they just make mistakes. IF they really are just out to make money (like Feel-Good Fakers—*Chapter 4*) from filmmakers, let karma do its job. Word will get around and the festival won't last.

Another expectation to keep in check is networking.

It's easy to be desperate that you'll meet a big-time agent, find a producer that will make your feature or discover the person you want to collaborate the rest of your life with.

You may, you may not.

You have no control over whom you meet, so let it go. Concentrate on enjoying yourself and promoting your film. Further, you don't know how the festival will stack up months down the line. It may SEEM like you met no one at that "lame" festival. But sometimes, that "lame" festival ends up having one audience member or person on the staff down the line that does something that opens a door. It has happened to me several times.

One time, there was a festival director who was high and couldn't figure out how to run the projector. I could have chosen to be annoyed or laugh.

I laughed.

We had a wonderful time as did everyone in the room . . . once he got the projector going.

The other thing to keep in mind is, festivals abroad are very different to attend than American ones and each country has a unique way they run things.

I find that American festivals are quite wonderful about pampering the filmmaker—swag bags, organizing events to network, showering us with compliments, yet they have other weaknesses—often they don't have large audiences (some do, this is not a blanket statement, but in general) and most of the time, your film only screens once.

Festivals abroad may never have one single networking event and many times there's no swag bag or caressing of ego—yet they usually have higher attendance, play your film several times during the festival and have a nice track record for taking your film to other places to screen after it's showed at theirs:

France's **Clermont-Ferrand Festival** took *Lunch Ladies* to two more festivals to screen—**La Criée Tout Court** in Marseilles and **SESIFF** (Seoul International Extreme-Short Image & Film Festival), and plan to take it to more festivals in the coming years.

Imagine Film Fest in Amsterdam screened the film at the

incredible Eye Museum, then took *Lunch Ladies* to **Lowlands Fest**, which is a huge event much like Coachella.

Portugal's **Motel X** took *Lunch Ladies* to **Shortcutz Network Viseu** and to more festivals across the country.

Filmets in Badalona, Barcelona went to **Sitges** and **Clermont-Ferrand** to scout films. They promoted *Lunch Ladies* at both places on their poster and the programmer also screened *Lunch Ladies* at important master classes to teach filmmaking students.

Strasbourg Fantastic Fest wanted to include *Lunch Ladies* in a special Halloween VR Screening to an international audience after it played at the festival. The film was unable to be part of this since I had already signed an exclusive French distribution contract, but the offer was there. A rew months later they also programmed the film as part of a special screening at Les Imaginales in Epinal.

Most festivals are great, just distinct, and it's pointless to regret spending money to go if your expectations are not met.

Throw expectations out and roll with the punches!

Check out my blog below where I learned SH*T HAPPENS and to be open to adventure!

SH*T HAPPENS

Writer/Producer Travels 1,850 Miles to See *The Lunch Ladies* in Mexico and Fails

The first screening mishap occurred because there was a Day of the Dead Parade and all the roads were blocked. The cabbie said he'd drop me off as close to the theatre as he could get me—i.e. on the side of the massive congested freeway where he pointed THAT WAY.

So, I got out and walked THAT WAY—Google Maps was self-imploding, so I panicked and started to run. Picture a chick in fishnets, combat boots and a dress battling a massive Day of the Dead crowd and armadillo floats. And yes, I'm not like a dude, I DID stop to ask three times if I was going the right way. "Si." Si my a*s! I was completely LOST!

Lungs burning from sprinting for 30 minutes straight, I started to sob. I realized I wouldn't make it. Then, it dawned on me, at least I could still get to the Q&A! I flagged another cab who wanted nothing to do with me but felt sorry for me—I really looked like hell by now. For an hour he attempted to beat the

Writer/Producer Clarissa Jacobson smiles on the red carpet 24 hours before failing massively to see the Lunch Ladies *international premiere at Latin America's top horror event—The Mórbido Festival.*

crazy traffic and just when we were getting close . . . wait for it . . . he got in an accident. So, I jumped out, ran some more and damn if I didn't find the theatre and just make it to the Q&A! Sweaty and stinky with mascara running down my face.

The second screening, I left my hotel 4 hours early. JUST IN CASE. At the theatre, with plenty of time to kill, I read emails, Instagrammed with some dude who tried to convince me he was Tré Cool from Green Day and had two gin and tonics. A half hour before the show, slightly buzzed and happy, I asked which theatre the film was playing in—"LO SIENTO—CANCELADO."

All I could do was laugh. Until it started to rain. At least I would see my friend Catya Plate's movie—*Meeting MacGuffin*. Right? WRONG! The Uber that picked me up from my CANCELADO film? Wait for it . . . he also got in an accident. So, I missed hers too!

I admit it, my annoyingly perky optimism was waning. I headed back to the hotel mulling over whether I should take one more chance and go see Gisberg Bermúdez Molero's film *El Silbón: Orígenes*. I had met him at the Opening Ceremony, and I wanted to support his work and see it.

It was my last night . . . I decided I should brush my teeth and go.

And then this happened.

That's when I said—"Mexico you have brought me to my knees! But hey, at least I got a cool Mórbido Swag Bag, got to walk the red carpet and go to a killer opening ceremony."

See? Sh*t happens, yet you can still have fantastic memories. I laughed so much about that trip it has become one of my favorite festival experiences ever.

Fantastic Mórbido Fest swag bag.

Further, after the fest, I connected with Gisberg, the director of *Él Silbon*. We discovered

Marvelous Mórbido Fest Opening Ceremony. (Photo credit: Robert Beltran for Mórbido Fest.)

we are on the same artistic page and plan to collaborate on projects in the future.

I can't help but smile and get warm fuzzies when I think of the Mórbido Festival.

Speaking of warm fuzzies . . .

LOVE THE Q&A

Your film has just been screened, the lights come up and now it's time for you to go on stage for Q&A.

"I HATE THE Q&A! I hate being in front of people, I don't wanna do it!"

Really?

You have a film in a flipping festival. So many people would love to be in your position. Be thankful you get to talk about it in front of an audience that wants to hear about it.

Love the Q&A!

I admit I didn't always love it. The first festival I slunk up to the front, embarrassed and shy. Partly because I wasn't sure they had liked the film and partly because I didn't want to be the center of attention. At the same time, I was busting with excitement but didn't want to show my excitement. Be cool, be cool . . .

That same night I went to another screening and saw someone else slink up to the stage for Q&A just like me and "be cool."

That's when it clicked:

No one wants to see someone go up on stage with their head down, face red, mumbling how they don't want to be looked at and hate being in front of an audience. Further, no one cares if you're cool or not, they just want you to be authentic. If you're excited, be excited. And, frankly, you should be excited.

If you aren't excited to talk about your film, no one is going to be excited about where it's going or where you're going. Excitement is infectious. If you are excited, the audience is excited, so be happy you are going up there to talk about your film!

"But I don't like to talk in front of people about my film, I really don't . . ."

First of all, that's nonsense. I never met a filmmaker who didn't want to talk about their movie. You know you want to, so talk about it and stop trying to act like you're so modest. You're not; you're acting pretentious. On the other side of the coin—no one wants to listen to someone who is all about themselves and how awesome they are and won't shut up. Share the floor.

Second of all, even if you're shy, that's okay! You'll work at it and get over it. There are so many things I was not good at during this process, so I got good at them. You'll get good too. A lot of doors will open for you if you trust you can get good at things you weren't good at before like . . .

NETWORKING

Networking wasn't always easy for me. Once, I even had to invite my sister to an event with me to be my wing woman because I was afraid to go and mingle by myself. She was always good at that kind of stuff.

Anyhow, over the years, I practiced. I became more at ease and learned to just go with the flow, introduce myself, ask questions, get people to talk about themselves, listen, and not give a care whether someone was impressed by me or not (that took a lot of pressure off). Now I have no problem and actually enjoy it.

I tell you this in case you struggle with it because it doesn't come naturally to everyone; it's hard for a lot of people. And there will be those at the festival that feel the same as you do. One thing is for sure at a film festival though, everyone loves film.

If you ask someone about their short or about what movies they saw that night that they liked, you will almost always get warmth and interest back, and before you know it you will be on to deeper conversation.

Also, I believe it doesn't matter WHO you network with. Talk to everyone.

You never know who knows someone, who will support you or who will help you. Yet, I see people all the time who only beeline for the biggest celeb, filmmaker or agent.

Yes. It's important to meet those people and talk about your project.

However, I can't tell you how many times the person who seemed like they had nothing going on, who wasn't even IN the industry who was wearing jeans and a t-shirt and downing a shot and being loud and funny, actually KNEW someone who could help me.

And they went to bat for me.

You don't know who will help you. Or where they will be years from now. EVERYONE is important. Treat everyone as equal. Because we all are. And besides, you don't want to be another Hollywood jerk who thinks otherwise.

The best advice I can give about networking, though, is to just try and chill out about it, bring your sense of joy that you have about your project with you, and above all GO.

Go to the event even if you are terrified.

You will meet someone, and that someone may be important in your growth as an artist!

CHAPTER 9

ENGAGING YOUR FAN BASE

(fans rock)

Fans will help you in ways you can never imagine—I was always shocked by the kindness of people (this includes reviewers and bloggers, as well) that took the time to promote *Lunch Ladies* simply because they loved it.

How do you get fans to talk about your film and help you?

You INCLUDE them in your journey.

Promote them when they promote you, support their endeavors, thank them for their help (no-brainer, but people forget to say thank you sometimes), connect with them, answer direct messages, answer comments on social media, if you blog, you can write a blog about a fan or a reviewer if they do something that shouts-out the film, you can send them swag . . . there are all kinds of ways to give back to people that help you and make it a two-way street of giving vs. a one-way street of taking.

I thought of fans as part of my marketing team and never took for granted how lucky I was to have them in my corner. In exchange they gave me so much back:

People made GIFS, fan art, jewelry, pictures, food, posted the film on their social media pages, photoshopped the *Lunch*

Ladies as themselves, made videos, took photos of themselves and their pets in hairnets, sent funny or odd news stories that I could use to keep my posts more interesting . . . the generosity went on and on.[1]

I even had one fan from Instagram hitchhike 210 miles out of his way just to see us at the Tulsa American Film Festival! How insanely wonderful is that?

FANS WILL HELP YOU AND ARE A HUGE PART OF YOUR SUCCESS

The Garcia Sisters, Authors of the Night Owl Chronicles Book Series (thenightowlchronicles.com.au) dressed as Lunch Ladies.

Reviewers, Bitches of Horror as the Lunch Ladies *advertising their podcast/review (ttf13.com).*

---

1   John Spaziale, a terrific Johnny Depp impersonator I met on Instagram, did a video in full Depp attire for the *Lunch Ladies* which can be seen on the *Lunch Ladies'* YouTube Channel, he also set *Lunch Ladies* up with an account on the Russian social media giant—VK.

Maverick owned by Melissa Dina McCarty.

Miss Mimi Le Mieux of the Pixie Project (pixieproject.org).

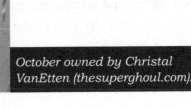

October owned by Christal VanEtten (thesuperghoul.com).

HOW DO YOU GET FANS?

Festivals. Tons from festivals.

But I also got fans another way.

I will tell you my secret: I shared a password protected link with anyone who asked me to see it. ANYONE. I didn't care if they were an eighteen-year-old kid in Ukraine, an Old Man in the Sea, or a real live Lunch Lady in good ole USA. Anyone who asked got to see it (with the exception of a few that gave me the heebie-jeebies).

My feeling was, how can I get fans if they have not seen the film and are not anywhere near a festival to view it? You can pique their interest with your promotion and your posts all you want, but until they've seen it, most are not going to promote it.

It is a risk to send the film to people you don't know and only you can decide if it's worth it. Some evil person CAN figure a way to post your short on social media or send it to all three hundred of their friends without your permission. However, I chose to believe the folks out there that love indie film and actually reach out to see it, would never do this—they are in the business of supporting filmmakers, not tearing them down.

And, guess what? They pulled through for me!

I sent the film to over one hundred strangers over the course of the run and not one betrayed my trust by stealing it or posting it somewhere.

The way I handled it was: If someone asked me to see it, I'd send them a password protected link and explain the situation about sharing. I'd also make sure the film was not download-able. I'd further change the password every week and tell them they had a limited time to see it and if they missed the window to hit me up for the new password.

I also made sure I emailed it to them and did not send it on direct message. That way I had a record of where it was going and I could reach out to them if they liked it and ask for help down the line—for example when the film got distribution, I reached out to all the folks who saw it and loved it and let them know they could now see it online.

Lastly, I'd ask that if they liked it, to rate it on IMDb, share on social media, whatever way they could help. No pressure, just a simple hey if you like it and feel inclined please support and do one or all or any of the following. If you don't ask for what you want, most won't think to do it, so ask and be amazed . . . so many helped me!

I would also carefully watch my social media; if someone was liking the posts a lot even though they hadn't seen it, I'd reach out, thank them and ask if they'd be interested in checking the film out.

It is exhausting sending your password protected film one by one to each person, but it pays off. If you decide to do it, keep track of who sees it on your Viewing Grid, their reactions, and if you get a great quote from them, ask if you can post it on social media and your website!

DISCLAIMER—*I take no responsibility if sh*t happens. It's a risk to send your film to a stranger; I can only tell you that it worked out for me.*

FELLOW FILMMAKERS

Filmmakers are your allies and will be the biggest fans you have.

They will promote you, support you and even hook up screenings or recommend your film to programmers they have worked with before.

For example, *Lunch Ladies* screened at **Nightmares Film Festival** along with Brooklyn Ewing's feature *She Was So Pretty: Be Good For Goodness Sake*, Mike Lombardo's *I'm Dreaming Of A White Doomsday* and Jeff Frumess' *Romeo's Distress*. We all became fast friends.

Brooklyn, later on, took *Lunch Ladies* to several conventions to screen with her feature—**Days of the Dead** in Indiana, **Space Jam Multimedia Festival** in West Virginia, and she further hooked up a screening for it at the **Skyline Drive-In**, also in Indiana.

Mike was in charge of **Scares That Care**—a charity film fest in Virginia—and screened it there. Mike also writes for the entertainment website called the Horror Syndicate, so he did a review and also had me on their podcast.

Jeff had a podcast called **Little Talk Of Horrors** and had me on as well.

There were so many more!

I met the fantastic Deborah Voorhees, filmmaker, director, writer and actress from *Friday 13th, A New Beginning* on Instagram. She reached out to me, told me *Lunch Ladies* sounded fun and asked if she could see it.

I sent her a link, she gave me an incredible review to post, then we talked on the phone—she shared a lot of great advice. She further put in a word for the *Lunch Ladies* at **Idaho Horror Festival** (which we got in) to the programmers telling them to watch for it. Lastly, she included a *Lunch Ladies* booth as part of the set design for a convention scene for her new film *13: Fan Boy.*

Rakefet Abergel, creator of *Jax In Love* and *Boo* loved *Lunch Ladies* and knew the women who run Reel Ghouls podcast— she hooked up an interview for me and a review.

Josh Hyde, Director/Writer/Producer of *My Friend's Rubber Ducky*—I met him at another fest several years before I made *Lunch Ladies*. Josh reached out after hearing about the film and had me on his "American Filmmaker Podcast."

At **deadCenter Festival** I met director/writer Joel Blacker. He introduced me to his team including actor/filmmaker Torrey Drake. Torrey runs a great little festival in Los Angeles called **Unreasonable Shorts**. Joel said, *"Hey, Torrey, you need Lunch Ladies in that fest."* Double whammy! Both Joel and Torrey hooked that up.

Shall I keep going? Okay two more.

Ruby Challenger, of the short *Daily Bread*, is an Aussie whom I met on Instagram when our films got in **Flickerfest**. Even though I couldn't make it to Australia, I had photos to use for promo as Ruby went to our screening, took pics and sent them to me! Further, she designed posters for another short of mine **A Very Important Film**.

I met Catya Plate, filmmaker of *Meeting MacGuffin*, at HollyShorts. She gave me so many leads for fests to submit to that I wasn't aware of—including Mórbido Fest—our international premiere. Catya also attended the lovely **Fano Film Fest** in Italy where both our films won. I couldn't go so she accepted *Lunch Ladies'* award for Best International Short and Best Actresses, read my thank you note to the audience and brought the trophy all the way back to the USA, then mailed it to me!

There were so many filmmakers that shared my *Lunch Ladies* posts, liked my social media, voted for the film in contests and more. It's incredibly refreshing to find out that most filmmakers in the indie community are not competitive, but supportive!

So be supportive . . .

DON'T BE A JERK!

Most filmmakers rock, but yes, there are jerks.

You don't wanna be a jerk, because no one is a fan of a jerk. How do you tell a jerk filmmaker?'

1. *They talk nonstop about their film but never ask you about yours.*

2. *They ask for a link to your film and never watch it.*

3. *They hated your film and instead of telling you what*

they liked about it (and there is <u>always</u> something to like) they will give you the silent treatment.

4. *They think their film is "precious," so they don't trust you with a link to see it. They advise you to check it out when it goes online or begrudgingly send it to you with a thesis explaining why not to share it.*

5. *They tell you they will shout-out, positively review or vote for your film. They never do.*

6. *They are unable to congratulate someone who got in a festival they didn't, got nominated when they didn't or won when they didn't. Yep, they're a jerk.*

7. *They think they are superior because their film is in the competitive section and yours isn't, so they are super cliquey and only hang with other jerk filmmakers in the competitive section.*

8. *They go to see their "masterpiece" and leave immediately after it's done missing everyone else's film in the block. For bonus points, they'll bring a jerk posse who will all get up and leave with them.*

9. *They give you a pseudo-compliment on your film like "I liked it . . . it was loud."* [2]

FINALLY, NUMERO TEN!

I love to rant about this so much, it needs its own special headline:

> **A JERK WILL GIVE YOU A CRITIQUE ON YOUR FILM . . .**
> **EVEN THOUGH YOU DIDN'T ASK FOR IT.**

---

[2] No lie, I got that "compliment" from a jerk filmmaker. And yes. *Lunch Ladies* is loud and his film is pretentious. So, we're even.

What purpose does unsolicited negative feedback on a finished product serve?

- *Do they think you will remember their critique for your next film and avoid mistakes? You are forever in their debt!*
- *Do they think they will have a huge impact on your creative life, much the way a trusted mentor would? Maybe they should be your mentor!*
- *Do they think you will thank them at the Oscars because they gave you "genius" critique a decade ago? They are the reason for all your success!*

No, they are a jerk.

Further, the criticism that is coming from them is usually anything BUT genius.[3] If they had the answers to brilliant filmmaking, they wouldn't be at a film festival trying to get a career like you; they'd be filming on Sony's backlot and collecting a big paycheck.

If you ask for no-holds-barred feedback, fine, they aren't a jerk.

But otherwise, they need to keep that negative stuff to themselves. The film is finished. There is nothing you can do to fix it even if you AGREE with their feedback, which is just an opinion and therefore up for debate.

Look for what is right in someone's film, not what is wrong (we have critics for that). Support other filmmakers; don't be a jerk.

Filmmakers will be your biggest fans if you are not a jerk!

---

[3] One dude I met on the circuit who had a realistic, dramatic "important" film decided to tell me he thought one of the characters in *Lunch Ladies* was over the top (obviously he did not understand the genre at all). I simply ignored his unsolicited critique and told him I loved his film (which I did). But, yes, I will always think of him as a jerk.

CHAPTER 10

THE FINAL MILE

(bewildering stuff you may have to deal with)

CREDIT

I'm not talking about running up the plastic, though that could be what happened when you made your film; I'm talking about credit in festival programs and publications.

If you're a director, you can skip past this section because you are not going to have any of the frustration that I did. However, if you are like me, a writer who made a film and chose not to direct, I am going to share my journey of constantly having to demand that my work be recognized, why I fought, how I won and why you must fight too.

IN THE BEGINNING

I was naive.

I thought that if I came up with the concept for my film, slaved over writing the feature for over a year, then the short, financed it with my own money, produced it, hired the director who had never heard of me or my script before then, found the majority of the cast and crew, dealt with locations, costuming, catering, paperwork, was the first on set, last to leave, did all the promotion, had sleepless nights over it, entered and attended festivals, did interviews . . . that the film would have my name on it.

IN THE MIDDLE

I discovered the painful truth.

I would open the festival program, and *Lunch Ladies* would be listed as a film BY the director. Nowhere would my name fall. Same for reviews . . . if I looked at a review the person would call *Lunch Ladies* the director's film.

I was confused, hurt, upset . . .

Furious.

IN THE END

I decided to ask programmers and publications to put my name on my film.

This was not easy.

I didn't want festival programmers to get mad at me. I didn't want reviewers to be annoyed. I didn't want to seem ungrateful. I didn't want to cause more work for people. I didn't want to ask two, three, four times until they did it. I didn't want people to think I had a huge ego. I did not want to rock the boat!

Yet, I could not live without the film having my name on it.

Not only was it incorrect, but it was not good for my career. [1]

So, I pulled my big girl pants on and asked and asked and asked.

---

[1] Why didn't I just direct? Well, kids, I wrote *Lunch Ladies*, produced it and was working a nine-to-five job at the time. That's enough! Furthermore, at the time I wasn't passionate about directing and I think too many people try to do too many things—film is a collaborative art; if you are writing, producing, directing, acting, editing, filming . . . something suffers. I didn't want anything to suffer. So, I found a fantastic director—J.M. Logan—to direct, and I handled the writing and majority of producing.

PROLOGUE

> **99% of festivals and 100% of reviewers added my name to the film.**

Some festivals fought me, and one refused me. Shame on them for clinging to a system that dates back to the auteur theory claiming the director is the sole author of the film. No one is the sole author—it takes a world of people to make a great film, not just the director. And if I've offended anyone by disrespecting the auteur theory, too bad; I've been offended by that theory (not fact, but THEORY) for years.

So . . . if you are in the same boat I am . . .

Ask.

When you are afraid to ask like I was, you can take my father's advice which helped me so much during this time:

"Whenever things are hard . . . ask yourself if you are in the right. If you are in the right, then fight."

> **You are in the right! FIGHT!**

BONUS SIDENOTE—*When you fill out the info on the platforms which are short-sighted as well—they will only ask for director bios. Put yours right up there next to his/hers. If you are truly the vision behind the film, you should be there too and any director worth his/her salt will support you. Mine (J.M. Logan) did. If you get in a festival who prints bios in their program, do the same; demand yours is there next to the director's.*

SALES REPS

What IS a sales rep? I didn't know either, so don't feel stupid.

A sales rep works like an agent. They will try to sell your film to distributors. Wait, what's a distributor? A distributor gets your film in front of an audience. Canal+, Amazon Prime Video, Netflix, Kanopy, Shorts TV, and Telemundo are all examples of companies that have distribution arms and buy films to carry on their channels.

They get their content mostly from sales reps.

Sales reps find their content—YOUR FILM—at festivals, on-line, word-of-mouth and all different kinds of ways. They get a commission for every deal they broker and have many relation-ships with distributors. They know what is hot in the market, and this drives the films they choose to represent.

They take a percentage of each sale, do all the work selling it, go to the festivals that have buyers, sign all the contracts, handle collecting the money, then send you an itemized list of what you have earned and pay you.

For most of us, if a sales rep knocks on our door, we are a little terrified.

We don't know IF we should trust them (we've all heard the horrible stories of sales reps who sell our film to a distributor and we never see a dime), if we should try to broker the deals ourselves and keep all the cash, and we certainly don't under-stand all this confusing legalese about what these people own and don't own if we sign with them.

I knew jack about it.

But I had to learn because I had one knock on my door pretty early on. And I almost turned down the best sales rep ever be-cause I didn't know anything. Luckily, they wouldn't take *"no"* for an answer, gently told me why I should be with them and very clearly explained the process to me.

DISTRIBUTION

TERRITORIES

A sales rep will sell your film to what are called "territories."

This is simply the part of the world the distributor covers: France, Spain, Korea, Mexico—these are all territories. You can have your film distributed in many territories, none or some.[2] Some distributor's territories include more than one country. For example, one may bundle France, Monaco, Switzerland and African countries into one territory.

Ideally, you want your film to be sold in as many territories as possible all over the world. The more places it is seen and distributed the bigger everyone's checks will be.

EXCLUSIVITY

The sales rep will broker either exclusive or non-exclusive deals. And if you don't have a sales rep, you want to make sure you know what type of deal you are signing with a distributor. Is it exclusive or non-exclusive?

> **For it to be exclusive, it better be worth it.**

For example, let's say Mars Central wants to carry your film for two years and they don't want any other competition (especially Uranus United whom they are at war with). They should pay a premium price or give a huge benefit to getting the exclusive deal because they are preventing your film from being screened by any other outlet in that territory.

A non-exclusive deal gives you more freedom but maybe less upside. Non-exclusive deals usually pay less as the film can be seen in other outlets they are in competition with.

---

2 This is another good reason to be in foreign festivals and collect your subtitles. If you have subtitles, it's easier down the line for a rep to get your film distributed internationally.

COST

A short film sales rep will generally take an agreed percentage of whatever is made.

On a feature film, it's less but you cannot compare a short to a feature—a short has a lot less market value which means a lot less cash so most sales reps have to work a lot harder to make money. Therefore, they will often take thirty to forty percent. Some take more, some take less. You must do the research and find out why your rep is charging more (maybe they will also be covering the cost of your film fest entries) or less (maybe they have tons of clients and won't spend much time on your film).

Whatever it costs. . . .

Is it worth it to hire a sales rep if they come knocking on your door?

Why should you give anybody one dime for something you could do yourself?

For the same reason I did:

1. *You don't want to deal with contracts or distributors. You are too busy, and besides, you don't understand all that boring legal stuff anyhow.*

2. *You don't have any clue who is buying short films. Your sales rep does. That's all they do 24/7 is build relationships with people who distribute films. Therefore, a sales rep will give you more opportunity at distribution than you could ever get yourself because they know whom to go to and who would want to buy your film. You don't. Unless of course, you've been studying this kind of stuff.*

3. *Let's just say you have been studying this kind of stuff—you know every distributor on the planet and*

what films they want to license. Unfortunately, you will discover that many distributors won't even take your call. This is because there are tens of thousands of short films out there every year and some distributors weed out content by only taking recommendations from sales reps they work with. The door is closed to you, but open to your sales rep.

4. *You don't want to chase distributors to send you money. You've licensed your film to a distributor in Antarctica.[3] Everyone there, especially the penguins, love it and watch it constantly. You've made bank. However, the distributor hasn't sent you your cut; they're pocketing it all for themselves. With an honest sales rep (and there are crooked ones out there too so you must do your due diligence), they're going to make sure you get your money. They will fight the distributors; you don't have to.*

5. *The more successful the film gets the more people will contact you about screening it. They will commit highway robbery if they can, giving you no upside—either paying you nothing or getting no eyeballs on the film. Your sales rep doesn't have time for that. Someone wants to carry your film and emails you? You don't have to look at their website and track record to see if it's worth your while. You dump it in your sales rep's lap and let them do the research.*

6. *You have a ton of contracts in place in many different territories. Mars wants to distribute your film. You are excited! Martians are amazing fans. You let them screen it. And then you remember you already signed*

---

3   *Lunch Ladies* WAS distributed in Antarctica! The penguins loved it.

a contract with Uranus that says you cannot screen on Mars. Yikes! Mars and Uranus are always at war! You are in breach of your contract! If you had a sales rep, you wouldn't have to worry about any of that; they keep track of it all.

As you can see, I think a sales rep is flipping worth it. Others may not. Only you know your answer. But for me, I wanna be an artist. Not an accountant.

HOW DO I KNOW IF MY SALES REP IS LEGIT?

You don't, so you must do research.

Understand the contract you are signing. Read every line—what you don't know, ask. There is someone out there you know who will be able to explain it to you. For things that are hazy, or you are unsure of? Ask the rep to clarify and make sure you understand.

> **Know what you are signing and what is required of you!**

Next, go to the rep's website. Find out who their clients are and call a few. Ask them if they've gotten paid. Ask them if the rep has done a good job and if they like working with them. Filmmakers will tell you the truth. If they haven't seen a dime or the rep doesn't return emails or sits around and does nothing, they'll tell you how they can't get out of their contract and wish they had never signed with them.[4]

With my rep, I called someone I met at a festival that signed with them that I trusted. They had nothing but good things to say. Do your due diligence and you will make the right choice.

---

4   *Lunch Ladies* director, J.M. Logan, gave me that terrific advice—thank you!

THE TEN COMMANDMENTS

Well, kids, all must good things must come to an end, so what better way than to recap everything I dumped on you with some fire and brimstone.

Please enjoy this sacrilegious cheat sheet you can carry at all times on your festival run:

1. *Thou shalt love and believe in thy film.*

2. *Thou shalt have a goal.*

3. *Thou shalt be prepared.*

4. *Thou shalt work hard.*

5. *Thou shalt love to promote thy film.*

6. *Thou shalt love to promote others.*

7. *Thou shalt not take rejection personally.*

8. *Thou shalt temper expectations.*

9. *Thou shalt be perseverant.*

10. *Thou shalt not be a jerk. Ever.*

AMEN

ABOUT CLARISSA

(who the heck is Clarissa?)

Clarissa is a screenwriter, voice-over artist, actress, and producer of her own content who is originally from Minnesota—land of sky-blue waters, tater-tots, and the best State Fair in the world!

A graduate of *Indiana University* and the *American Musical and Dramatic Academy* in New York City, Clarissa started as a performer and later discovered her true passion—screenwriting. From there, she joined *Twin Bridges Writing Salon*—the longest running workshop in Los Angeles—helmed by her mentor Joe Bratcher and his wife Judy Farrell.

At *Twin Bridges*, she exorcised the crazy character voices in her head and penned several scripts—including the murderous, conniving, yet strangely loveable *Lunch Ladies*.

Lunch Ladies is a quirky comedy/horror about two high school *Lunch Ladies* who do whatever it bloody takes on their quest to become Johnny Depp's personal chefs. After hearing Hollywood suits say *"it's funny but there's no market for it"* she decided to write a short based on the feature, produce and finance it and prove them wrong.

And . . . well . . . she did!

The short went to over 100 film festivals, won thirty-eight awards to date, and secured distribution all over the world on

Amazon's Prime Video, France's Canal+, Kanopy and more. Her journey with the film became the catalyst for this book.

In addition, Clarissa also recently created another short—A Very Important Film—which is a five-minute mockumentary about a woman named Clarissa who made a short named *Lunch Ladies* and realized it wasn't important and has now made something important. It's her commentary on the prevalent snobbery that exists in the film world, which often ignores genre and comedy films thinking they aren't important.

They are.

Ms. Jacobson currently resides in Los Angeles with all the other beautiful weirdos.

Contact Clarissa at:

heyimclarissaj.com

Made in the USA
Columbia, SC
29 September 2020